AL SCHMITT
ON THE RECORD

AL SCHMITT

ON THE RECORD

THE MAGIC BEHIND THE MUSIC

AL SCHMITT

WITH MAUREEN DRONEY

ROWMAN & LITTLEFIELD
Lanham • Boulder • New York • London

Published by Rowman & Littlefield
An imprint of The Rowman & Littlefield Publishing Group, Inc.
4501 Forbes Boulevard, Suite 200, Lanham, Maryland 20706
www.rowman.com

6 Tinworth Street, London SE11 5AL, United Kingdom

Originally published in hardcover by Hal Leonard Books in 2018

British Library Cataloguing in Publication Information Available

Library of Congress Cataloging-in-Publication Data Available for the Hal Leonard Books edition.

Names: Schmitt, Al, author. | Droney, Maureen.
Title: Al Schmitt on the record : the magic behind the music / Al Schmitt with Maureen Droney.
Description: Montclair, NJ : Hal Leonard Books, 2018. | Includes index.
Identifiers: LCCN 2018033584 | ISBN 9781495061059 (cloth : alk. paper) | ISBN 9781538137666 (pbk : alk. paper)
Subjects: LCSH: Schmitt, Al. | Sound recording executives and producers—United States— Biography.
Classification: LCC ML429.S337 A3 2018 | DDC 781.49092 [B]—dc23
LC record available at https://lccn.loc.gov/2018033584

To my wife, Lisa, and to my children,
Al, Karen, Stephen, Chris, and Nick

CONTENTS

FOREWORD

by Sir Paul McCartney

WHEN I WORKED with Al and Tommy LiPuma on my *Kisses on the Bottom* album we would do a take, and when we had one that we thought was good enough, we'd go into the control room to check it. This was always a revelation for me because Al had transformed the take into a great-sounding record. This is a skill that very few recording engineers have.

The various techniques that Al uses are a mystery to me and it's such a joy to be working with someone who understands this magical process. Al would tell us stories of his experiences with everyone from Jefferson Airplane to Frank Sinatra and many other great artists. This encouraged me to share stories of my own, so the sessions were often more like social events than work.

More than all of this, Al is a great human being who cares deeply about what he does and the people he works with. He is admired by many recording artists and fellow engineers for these qualities.

I always wished I knew more about Al and so am very much looking forward to reading this book. Thank you, Al, for the wonderful times we have shared.

Love,
Paul

ACKNOWLEDGMENTS

Sᴘᴇᴄɪᴀʟ ᴛʜᴀɴᴋs ᴛᴏ

Tom Dowd, Bob Doherty, Paula Salvatore, Niko Bolas, Phil Ramone, Tommy LiPuma, Steve Genewick, Bill Smith, and my friends and partners in METAlliance: Ed Cherney, Elliot Scheiner, George Massenburg, Chuck Ainlay, and Frank Filipetti.

AL SCHMITT
ON THE RECORD

1

BUT I'M NOT QUALIFIED, MR. ELLINGTON!

———

I WAS NINETEEN and just out of the navy when I started working at Apex Recording Studio on West Fifty-Seventh Street in Manhattan. Located on the second floor of the Steinway Building, it was a big room that sounded great. On the first floor of the building was the Steinway & Sons showroom.

In those days, jazz was the hottest thing happening in New York, and Apex had a reputation as the best place to record it. It was a top-notch studio, and getting a job there turned out to be a very lucky break for me—especially because, as it happened, Tom Dowd was working there as an engineer. Tommy was only a few years older than I was, and it was pretty early in his career. But he'd already done a lot of recording and was starting to make a name for himself.

It was my Uncle Harry who had recommended me for the job. Harry was a well-known recording engineer, and starting from when I was a little kid, I'd spent time helping out at his studio and learning the recording ropes. He knew that I was just out of the service and back home in New York, trying to figure out what to do next. He was also good friends with the owner of Apex, and when he heard about a job opening there, he put in a good word for me. I went for an interview and was hired as an apprentice. At the beginning, my job was mostly to help out on the sessions Tommy Dowd was doing, following him around and learning how things should be done.

After about three months, the studio manager thought I'd learned enough to take on some of the work that we called "little demo dates." They were pretty simple. People would come in with a song they'd written, to play piano and sing the song. Or a guy might come in to have himself recorded singing a song that he liked as a gift for his girlfriend. It was all mono, of course. We recorded on ten- or twelve-inch lacquer discs, depending on the length of the song, and we cut at 78 rpm. We'd set the level, run the lathe, and cut a disc. Then we'd put it in a sleeve, collect the fifteen-dollar payment, and the customers would leave with something that they could play at home. The disc was pretty fragile, so they couldn't play it forever. But if they were careful, they'd get quite a few spins out of it.

After I'd gotten a few of these dates under my belt, my boss thought I was doing well enough to come into the studio by myself on a Saturday, while the rest of the staff was off for the weekend, and record the demo sessions that were booked for that day. It was my first Saturday at the studio, and my first time there alone. But we had a schedule book that listed who was coming in, and there was a receptionist downstairs in the Steinway showroom who would let me know when a client was coming up.

It seemed simple enough, so I wasn't worried. According to the book, I had three people coming in, one at ten a.m., one at noon, and one at two p.m. I got there early and was set to go when the first person came in at ten. He played guitar and sang "Happy Birthday" to his daughter, I recorded him, and that was it. The noon session was a guy who played piano and had written a song. I put a mic on him and a mic on the piano, got the balance while he ran it through, and then cut his disc.

When that was done, I waited for my two o'clock, which was, according to the book, someone named Mercer. I liked to meet the clients when they arrived, and so would stand by the elevator where I could greet them as they got off. Then I'd take them into the studio. So, when the receptionist buzzed a few minutes before two to say that my client was on the way up, I was ready and waiting at the elevator for Mr. Mercer.

But when the big brass elevator doors opened up in front of me, five guys came walking out carrying instrument cases. One of them asked me where the studio was.

I said, "The studio is right here, sir. But we're booked, we have a session."

The one who'd spoken laughed and said, "You're waiting for Mercer, right?"

"Yeah, that's right," I answered.

"That would be Mercer Ellington," he replied. "We're here to record with the Mercer Ellington band. Duke will be here, too."

I must have turned white with shock, because, instantly, fear overtook me. I honestly felt like my heart was going to stop beating. I was a bebopper; I loved jazz and big bands. I understood what was supposed to happen and who these guys were, but I had absolutely no idea what to do about it. Some of the musicians coming out of the elevator carrying their instruments were my heroes. They were the virtuosos, the players from Duke Ellington's band, like Billy Strayhorn on piano and the great Johnny Hodges on saxophone. For this session, they were going to be working with Mercer Ellington, Duke's son.

What I learned later was that Duke and Mercer, along with the famous and very influential jazz critic Leonard Feather, were partners in a label they called Mercer Records. As it turned out, all three of them were going to be there that day for the session.

Standing there, looking at the musicians' expectant faces, I started stuttering, "Oh, no, no, no, there's been a mistake! This isn't the session that's supposed to be here. Please, wait a minute while I check on this."

I turned, ran into the office and got on the phone. I called Tommy Dowd first, but I couldn't reach him. Then I called my boss but I couldn't reach him, either. Now I was in full panic mode. What was I going to do?

Then I remembered that I had my book. It was a little notebook that Tommy had given me where I could draw diagrams of his setups every time he did a session. I'd mark what mics he used and where he put the instruments and the mics. I asked one of the musicians how many instruments there were, and he said, "It's a big band. We have four trumpets, four trombones, five saxophones, and the rhythm section.

More musicians were arriving, so I got out my book, raced into the studio and started setting up. There were no vocals, just instruments, and we only had eight inputs on the console, which meant I only had eight microphones to place. In the studio, the musicians were starting to get it together, talking and looking over their charts. My heart was pounding, but I managed to get the studio set up the way I remembered seeing Tom do it. I did what I could with the microphones, looking at my book and putting them where I thought they should be.

Then, Duke Ellington walked in. I'd seen him perform many times, and I recognized him immediately; I remember he had wavy, pomaded black hair and was dressed in a nice brown suit.

I went up to him and said, "Mr. Ellington, I'm sorry, but this is a big mistake. I'm not qualified to do this! They didn't expect this kind of session when they booked it, so I'm the only person working today. And I'm only allowed to do little things."

"Well," he replied. "Don't worry, son. The setup looks fine, and the musicians are out there."

At that point, there was really no choice to be made. I went into the control room and started opening up the mics, and Duke came in and sat next to me. He could see I was trembling, and probably thought I was about to collapse. I just kept repeating, "Mr. Ellington, I'm not qualified, really I'm just not qualified."

But he was very kind. He just stayed calm and listened. Finally, he patted me on the arm and said again, "Don't worry, son. We're going to get through this. You're going to do great, and things are going to be just fine." So, I kept on going and he kept telling me that all the way through.

And we did get through it; and it was all right. In three hours, we cut four songs. I couldn't tell you today what the names of the songs were, but they really did sound just fine.

I can't describe how much relief I felt when it was over. Later, I told Tommy Dowd that if I'd known the night before that this session was going to happen—that it was a big band, and that Duke Ellington himself was going to be there—I would have called in sick. I'd have told them to get somebody else to do it. But instead, I found myself in the middle of it. I had to do it, it came out okay, and that gave me a big shot in the arm. It boosted my confidence immensely. And from then on, because I'd done it—I'd gotten through the session and it was all right—my boss started letting me do more. I was on my way.

2

THE BEGINNING:
EARLY DAYS, NEW YORK, NEW YORK

I'VE BEEN IN the recording studio since I was seven years old. That's the truth. My uncle, my father's brother Harry Smith, had a studio and was a very well-known recording engineer. He'd opened his studio in the 1930s. Because of the anti-German sentiment in that era—the run up to World War II—he'd changed his name from Schmitt to Smith, and the studio was called Harry Smith Recording. It was at 2 West Forty-Sixth Street and, on weekends, I'd go over and hang out. I was just a little kid, but there I was, on the subway by myself from Brooklyn to Manhattan, where I'd spend the weekend watching him record.

Young Al Schmitt with his sister, Doris.

MY UNCLE'S STUDIO: LESSONS IN LIFE AND STYLE.

The visits had started back when I was very small. My father would take me with him when he went to see Harry, who, in addition to being my uncle, was also my godfather. I was just tagging along, but Harry had no children of his own, so he'd take me out for ice cream sundaes and treat me as if I was his own son.

Finally, starting when I was eight, I was able to, on a Saturday, by myself, get on the subway and go to visit his studio. People allowed that back in those days. You wouldn't let an eight-year-old do that now, but back then, it was safe.

I'd get off at the Forty-Seventh Street station, spend the day at the studio, and then stay over Saturday night at Harry's place. He was everything in the world I admired at that time. He was successful—and famous—as an engineer, and he always carried a big wad of cash. I remember he'd always have one hundred dollars, which was a whole lot of money back then. And whatever he spent that day he'd replenish, so that he started out the next day again with one hundred dollars. He dressed well, he took me to the best restaurants, where he always got the best tables, and he was respected. He was an amazing guy and it was so much fun for me.

I'd watch him record big bands and I'd help out where I could. My jobs were to set up the chairs where he wanted them placed before the musicians arrived, and to clean the cables and generally keep things neat. I also had to stay out of his way. That was really important, because he moved around a lot and the control room was small. A lot of the time I had to figure out how to make it seem like I wasn't around at all.

There was only one microphone on the sessions, so the setup and placement of musicians was all-important to get everything sounding good. My uncle would move the musicians around to get the right balance. Then he'd make them take off their shoes so that they wouldn't make noises tapping their feet. When it was time for a solo, the musician whose turn it was would have to get up and go over to the mic.

I was just a wide-eyed kid and my uncle was my hero. I loved my mother and father, but life with Uncle Harry was glamorous. He had an apartment at the very prestigious One Beekman Place building near the river on Manhattan's East Side, and he drove a beautiful convertible. He had a great life, and that's who I wanted to be.

Harry Smith Recording was the first independent recording studio on the East Coast. One of its claims to fame was that Frank Sinatra had made his very first recording with a band there. As the story went, Frank happened to be at Harry's studio one day hanging out with a band that had come in to do a session. When the band finished all the songs they'd planned to record that day, there was still some time left over. Frank asked if they'd cut another tune and let him sing on it. They said yes, and he did. It was a never-released version of the song "One Love," which was later re-recorded by Frank as part of his Columbia Records repertoire. This story, of course, added to the cachet of the studio, which had also hosted many other jazz greats, including rare studio recordings by legendary saxophonist Charlie Parker that were made for Savoy Records, among them: 1947's "Cheryl," with the Charlie Parker Quintet: Parker, Miles Davis on trumpet, Max Roach on drums, Bud Powell on piano, and Tommy Potter on bass, and, in 1948, "Parker's Mood," with the Charlie Parker All Stars: Modern Jazz Quartet founder John Lewis on piano and Curley Russell on bass.

Tommy Potter, Charlie Parker, Max Roach, and Miles Davis
(from left to right). In New York, NY. (*William P. Gottlieb/Ira
and Leonore S. Gershwin Fund Collection, Music Division,
Library of Congress*)

Before he'd opened his own facility, Harry had worked for Brunswick Records, where he'd made some of the great records of the time, like Benny Goodman's "Sing, Sing, Sing." He knew all the musicians and was friends with them. He was also great friends with Les Paul.[1]

Harry and Les were both recording pioneers, and they worked on all sorts of projects and inventions together. They also hung out together, and they'd bring me along with them. That's another thing that's different now. Back then, kids were allowed in drinking establishments, so I'd go along with my father and my uncle and his friends. I was in bars a lot in those days! I'd get a sarsaparilla or a Coca-Cola while they enjoyed their adult beverages. The bartenders always treated me nicely, putting a cherry in my drink to make it special.

Les became like another uncle to me, and he liked to tease me. I loved to look stylish, and I wore my hair in a pompadour with a ducktail, so he always made sure to mess up my hair whenever he saw me. We stayed friends all his life and Les never stopped being irreverent; when I was inducted into the TEC Awards Hall of Fame in 1997, I introduced him to my wife, Lisa, and he said to her, "You're a heck of a lot prettier than the woman he was with last night!"

Tom Dowd, me, Stevie Wonder, and Les Paul at the TEC Awards
in 1997 when I was inducted into the TEC Awards Hall of Fame.
(*Courtesy of TEC Awards/Photograph by Alan Perlman*)

Uncle Harry was good at what he did and was always working—and hanging out with—the cream of the crop. The great jazz pianist Art Tatum had an office higher up in the same building, and on Saturdays, Art would come down to Harry's studio and rehearse on the piano. If I was there, he'd sit me next to him, take my hand, and show me boogie-woogie licks. I didn't know who Art Tatum was. I just thought he was a friendly black man with a great smile who treated me kindly.[2]

There were so many famous people in the studio, all of the time. Orson Welles would come by, and sometimes we'd talk. It was not long after his headline-making radio broadcast *War of the Worlds* and he asked me one day if I believed in Martians. I told him I didn't know and he just laughed and patted me on the head. There were the Andrews Sisters, Bing Crosby, all of the big stars of the day. Bing would talk to me and I still remember how he always smoked a pipe and how good it smelled; not that many people smoked pipes in those days—cigarettes or cigars were the norm.

To me, it was the most amazing place imaginable. Back in Brooklyn, my immediate family was very, very poor. My mother was seventeen when I was born and my sister Doris was born right after me. I had two younger brothers also, Richy and Russell, who, as it turned out, both became audio engineers as well.

So, we were four kids in all, and I don't think my father ever worked less than six days a week. I remember him making seventeen dollars a week. It wasn't enough, and there were times we didn't have enough food for all of us to eat.

Because at home we had so little, I thought my uncle was a millionaire. And every Sunday, when he put me back on the subway for home, he gave me a twenty-dollar bill—more than my father made working all week. I took that money and gave it to my mother. It was my uncle's way of helping my father, you see, without making my father feel like he was getting a handout.

My father was a very proud man who worked hard all his life, from making PT boats in the Brooklyn Navy Yard to working for a printing company and managing a record-pressing plant. He always had a job, but there was never enough money to go around. I loved and respected my father, but I wanted to be like Harry.

Something else that my uncle did for me that I think was very formative was that, when I was about eleven, he gave me a wind-up portable phonograph player and a stack of records. I especially recall some by Ella Fitzgerald with Chick Webb, the great jazz and swing drummer and bandleader: "I Want to be Happy," and "Hallelujah, I Love Him So."[3]

There was also a hit song by Ella Mae Morse that was one of my favorites, called "Cow, Cow Boogie." I'd bring the phonograph to school with me and a bunch of us would sit around in the evenings in the schoolyard playing records and digging the music. Some of the other kids would bring records they had at home; Woody Herman's "Caldonia" got a lot of play in that schoolyard. Or somebody would bring a radio and we'd listen to the great disc jockey Fred Robbins, who had a very famous show called *Robbins' Nest*. Fred broke a lot of pop records and artists like Mel Torme, Billie Holiday, and early Frank Sinatra. It was a really popular and influential show for people who loved music.

We'd dance the Lindy Hop and jitterbug and we'd end up with about fifteen or twenty people all listening and dancing. It was a wonderful thing and it kept us out of trouble. We weren't drinking or smoking weed. We just loved the music.[4]

Meanwhile, because we were so poor, I was also working. Some Saturdays, I shined shoes at a little shoe repair shop. I charged a quarter for a pair of shoes, and all the customers gave me tips. Other times, my mother and I would go to the bakery very early in the morning and buy big pretzels, two for a penny. My mother would make a pretty basket for them, lined with a nice white napkin, and we'd sell them for a penny a piece. We'd buy a dollar's worth of pretzels, and when we sold them all, we had two bucks—a 100 percent profit! I'd give a dollar back to my mother and the other dollar I got to keep.

Earning money was important to me—to help my family, but also to have nice things. I guess I got the desire for those nice things from my uncle, who was always beautifully dressed. Starting from the time I was eleven, I earned the money to pay for my own clothes. I was into style, and I wanted to wear the pegged pants that were all the rage, but my father was against my having them. It was kind of outside the norm, part of the zoot suit craze—high-waisted, wide-legged, narrow-ankle trousers. My father didn't like the idea, but he agreed that I could wear them if I was able to pay for them myself. And that's what I did.

I was into baseball as well, and it was the same with the first baseball glove that I really wanted. My father bought me a glove, but it wasn't the one I wanted. I had to work and save the money to buy that one. It cost four dollars, and boy, saving that four dollars took a long time.

I also saved up the money to buy the first record I knew I wanted to own. I was way into big bands and jazz by that time, and I loved the band leader Jimmie Lunceford. That first record I bought was one of his. It was a twelve-inch, 78 rpm vinyl record that had "Jazznocracy" on one side and "White Heat" on the other.[5]

The first record I bought, Jimmie Lunceford's "Jazznocracy" backed with "White Heat."

When I listened to that record, I'd remember seeing my uncle recording big bands, and somehow, it became what I wanted to do. I never really wanted to do anything else. I would close my eyes and pretend I was my uncle, being the engineer and moving my hands and fingers. I did that with a lot of records, but in particular with that one by Jimmie Lunceford. I could picture the band set up in front of me and myself doing the actual recording, with everyone telling me how good it was and making me feel really proud of myself.

My mother wanted me to be an electrical engineer. My father wanted me to be anything I wanted to be. But my uncle wanted me to be a recording engineer, and I knew I wanted that, too. That was pretty much the start of it.

From when I was eight until I was about thirteen, I spent most Saturdays at my uncle's studio. After a while, besides cleaning and setting up chairs, there were other things he'd have me do. For example, we didn't yet have tape recorders, so the recordings were still cut direct to acetate discs. Originally, the base of the acetate was aluminum, but once World War II started, the aluminum that was originally used in the process all went to the war effort. They had to figure out a substitute, and what they came up with was glass—the glass was the base of the disc, and the acetate was the top.

Acetate was highly flammable, and you had to be very careful when handling it. A mink-hair brush was attached to the cutting lathe to stop what we called the chip—the spiral cutout of acetate that was created as the disc went around. The operator, in this case my uncle, would have to take the chip off the disc and put it in a metal, fireproof container. We didn't have suction at that time to remove the chip, just a stylus that cut the groove. One of my jobs became to help my uncle brush the chip into the container while he was cutting a disc. It was actually quite difficult, because the glass base broke easily. That's one of the reasons I learned to always be extra careful in the studio, and to take very good care of the equipment. If a glass master broke, that was the end of that performance!

Something my uncle used to say that has always stuck with me was, "This equipment is very delicate. Take care of it and it will take care of you. You have to treat it like it's a Swiss watch and you're the watchmaker." All of the equipment was delicate in those days. Not like what we have today, where you can bang it around. If you did that then, it just wouldn't function!

3

LEARNING FROM THE GREATS

THINGS CHANGED for me when I got to be thirteen or so. Instead of spending time at my uncle's studio, I started hanging out with a bunch of wild kids and getting into trouble. They were stealing cars, making cash pickups for the local bookie, getting involved with robberies at the airport, all sorts of stuff. It was pretty much like an early version of *Goodfellas.* They were doing things to make money that were likely to end badly, and I began to realize that things might not turn out so well for me. I knew it was possible that I could end up in jail and I was worried about my future. I needed a means to get away from the bad stuff going on around me, so I decided to enlist in the United States Navy. And, when I graduated from high school at seventeen, that's what I did.

I spent two and a half years in the navy. And here's something funny. I was sent to boot camp at the naval station in Great Lakes, Illinois, near Chicago. They taught us how to shoot, and I had to learn how to use an M1 rifle. But when I was eleven, I'd had an accident that left me almost totally blind in my right eye. When I enlisted, during the physical exam I read the eye chart mostly with my good left eye, so that I passed my tests and got accepted. But when I got to boot camp, we were put on the firing range and were expected to shoot our rifles at targets that were one hundred yards away. There were marines standing behind us to show us how to do it. So, there I was, leaning over as far as I could to see out of my left eye. The marine behind me started laughing, then said, "You're going to get a heck of a score." I knew I wasn't doing well at all, so I said, "Really?" And he said, "Yeah, the guy next to you is shooting at your target." Turns

Here I am as a teenager with my sister, Doris.

out that guy was really good, and I got sharpshooter status. It went on my official navy record that way, so if anyone was looking for a sharpshooter, they'd say, "Get Schmitt!"

Luckily, I didn't have to use that rifle much. I was sent for communications training in Washington DC, where I worked with codes, and I stayed there the whole time I was in the service. It was actually pretty great because there was a lot of music going on in DC then. At the time, artists who had drug convictions, like Billie Holliday, lost their license to perform in New York and were banned from working in the city's cabarets. But they could work in Washington. There were some great jazz clubs there, and I got to see and hear a lot of my favorite performers on a regular basis.

APPRENTICESHIP: APEX AND FULTON RECORDING STUDIOS

When I got out of the service, it was 1950 and I was nineteen years old. I was planning to enroll at City College of New York, but I was home only two weeks when Uncle Harry called. A friend of his who owned a really good studio was booking a lot of great sessions. He needed someone he could break in for a job there, and Harry wanted to know if I was interested.

Was I interested? You bet! It was Apex Recording Studio, in the beautiful Beaux-Arts Steinway building across from Carnegie Hall. I met Bob Scheuing, the owner, for an interview and he said, "Come back Monday morning at nine o'clock. You've got the job."

THE STUDIO

My first day was Monday, March 1, 1950, and I got to Apex bright and early. Bob took me into the studio and introduced me to the two engineers who were already working there. One was a German guy with a monocle who actually clicked his heels when we met. His name was Fred Herbert Otto. And then, there was the other guy, the one I was to apprentice with. His name was Tom Dowd.[1]

The story of Tom Dowd, nuclear physicist turned recording engineer,
Tom Dowd & the Language of Music.

At that point, I had no idea who Tommy was. But he liked me right away and I became a kind of kid brother to him. I just jumped in his back pocket and followed him around. I was running errands and cleaning up and all that, but I also got to watch all of Tom's sessions. I got to see what mics he used and how he set up, and he bought me a little notebook so that I could write everything down and draw diagrams. It wasn't long before we also became good friends. We were both hockey fans and, twice a week when the Rangers played, we'd go to Madison Square Garden together and watch the games. Other times we'd go drinking and just hang out and talk.

I was still into big bands, and I was still a bebopper. I loved that kind of jazz: Chet Baker, Dizzy Gillespie, Billy Eckstine, Gerry Mulligan, John Coltrane, Miles Davis, all the greats, and the saxophone players like Allen Eager, Brew Moore, and the piano player Lennie Tristano. They took regular jazz off into avant-garde and that's what I was into. We all wore pegged pants and hung out in the clubs. Billy Eckstine wore shirts with a wide, spread collar that we called the "Mr. B" collar, so we all went out and bought Mr. B shirts. And we all wore our hair in a pompadour with a ducktail. It was a way of life that, fundamentally, was all based on the music.

Apex was doing almost all of the work for Atlantic, National, and Prestige, labels that were recording a lot of the musicians I admired. I was working at a studio where my idols, whose records I was buying and who I was going to clubs and paying my hard-earned money to hear, were coming in to record. I'd see them walk in and my mouth would drop open. I was getting to meet Erroll Garner, Dizzy Gillespie, Charlie Parker, and so many other great players. I couldn't believe this was happening to me. They were heroes. It was like getting to meet Joe DiMaggio and Babe Ruth, the greatest baseball stars of all time.

It was a whole scene and a lifestyle, too. I'd be cleaning up and there would be marijuana all over the place. I didn't use it, but I knew what it was. I was just watching everything around me, and like a blotter, I was sucking it all in. I was learning all the time.

Back then in New York when I started at Apex there weren't assistant engineers. There was one engineer on the session who did everything, from positioning the mics and balancing the sounds to cutting the discs on the lathe. At the time I arrived there, the studio didn't yet have a tape machine; we cut to two Presto lathes. It wasn't until a little while later that the studio got its first tape recorder: a mono Ampex 300. Then, the engineer had to run that tape recorder as well as the lathe!

There were no assistant engineers but, as the studio apprentice, I got to be on all the dates. Tom would show me how to do certain things, like which mics to use on what instruments, and how to set them up. We didn't have a lot of mic stands, so sometimes we'd have to just set the mics on chairs. We had mostly RCA 44 and 77-DX ribbon microphones, and a few Western Electric 639s—the "birdcage" mics, which had three patterns: unidirectional, nondirectional, and bidirectional.[2]

After the mics were set up, I'd watch how Tom would place the different groups—how he'd arrange and balance them around the microphones. He'd place the mics, go into the control room and listen, then run back out and move one musician back farther, or another musician in a little bit closer, until he got the right blend.

Tommy also taught me how to act in the studio. My uncle had taught me a lot, but working with him as a kid, I hadn't been outgoing; I waited for people to talk to me first. Tommy taught me that I should talk to the musicians and befriend them, instead of just being in awe of them and running back and forth without saying anything. I learned to be a lot friendlier and to be comfortable with the musicians and the singers, and I think that has helped my career a lot.

I can't recall if the first console I worked on at Apex was six inputs or eight but it was no more than that. Since you could only have six or eight microphones, we had to learn how to balance everything. That's where mic technique came in. For example, we might have to put the upright bass and the rhythm guitar on the same mic. Or sometimes we'd put the bass player on a riser, open the piano top, and have one mic that would catch both the piano and the upright bass. Then we'd have to move the bass player forward or back to find the position that captured the best balance between the two instruments.

I learned from both Tommy and my uncle how to do that kind of thing. With so few inputs, sometimes we didn't even put a mic on the drums. When we did, it was just one mic overhead.

I still remember one session I did in about 1951 with Tiny Kahn, a big-time drummer who died when he was only thirty. He had a little trio, so we only had three mics set up—one for each person—and he said to me, "Hey, kid, put a mic on the bass drum."

I said, "Are you kidding me? We don't do that."

He insisted, "Yeah, you gotta do it. It will give it a little of that tempo thunder thing."

I told him no; it was too radical. But he convinced me to give it a try, so I put an RCA 44 mic on the bass drum. And when I opened it up, it surprised me. It had a bit more punch that made the drum fit in really well along with the bass and piano. It was just a little thing, but it made it special. That sounds funny now, but remember, we were working with hardly any equipment. And everything was still all mono. No stereo.[3]

Since we only had the one studio at Apex, when Tommy was working I was always there helping him. Then, after a while, when he couldn't be there I started doing some of the sessions. Otto, the other engineer, did certain things, like recording radio shows for an account we had with Voice of America. But Otto was the day guy, and many of those shows were done at night. I didn't have a problem working late, so I ended up doing a lot of them, too.

We did the Voice of America shows in all sorts of languages. It was great experience. I did shows in Italian where we'd put two mics over the table, and two guys would just sit and talk. We also did full on radio shows where the actors would be working from scripts, with a sound effects guy there beside them creating the effects live. He'd make the sounds of horse's hooves with halves of coconut shells, crumple cellophane paper close to the mic to simulate fire, and use wooden blocks for the sound of marching men. There was even a water tank for splashing sounds.

A lot of people got their start on those radio shows, like actor Telly Savalas, who coined the phrase "Who loves you, baby?" and became famous starring on television in *Kojak*. Early in Telly's career, I worked with him and his family on a Voice of America show that was all in Greek.

We recorded the radio shows on sixteen-inch acetates that we called transcription discs. By then, the war was over and we were back to aluminum-based discs. You could fit an entire fifteen-minute show at 33 1/3 rpm on the discs, depending on the feed screw you were using. The feed screw was the manual screw that controlled how many lines per inch you could cut, and thus, how much time you got on the disc. There was no automatic way to change the amount of lines per inch. When we recorded 78s we would have either eighty-eight lines per inch, or up to 96. For sixteen-inch transcription discs at 33 1/3, it would be anywhere from 112 to 136 lines per inch; 136 allowed more time on the disc, because the lines were closer together, and 112 got less.

We called these transcription recordings air checks or air feeds. If the show started at 8:30 p.m., you'd get ready at 8:15, then just before 8:30 you'd drop the cutting head, throw the switch, and start recording the show. Afterward, you'd make copies for the artists, who'd pick them up the next day so they could listen to how it had sounded. The radio stations didn't do that for them, so we did.

It was usually a fifteen-minute show. The talent would run it down a couple of times, then we'd record. They'd be reading the script as we recorded. Sometimes they'd make mistakes and when they did, we'd have to start over from the beginning. Everything had to be done in one take, because with discs there was really no way to stop and start. We tried, though! Tommy and I experimented with some of the craziest things.

When we were recording music, normally, we'd put two or three takes on a sixteen-inch disc at 33 1/3. We'd have Take 1, 2, and 3 on one disc and on another one we'd have Take 4, 5, and 6. On one session, Tommy and the producer liked the beginning of Take 2 and the ending of Take 5, but, of course, they were on separate discs. So, we put together two turntables, found the right spots and marked the discs. Then we each played one of the discs; I played mine out while he played his in. The two turntables went into the console and then on to the cutting lathe. There we were, doing disc-to-disc editing!

Other times, we'd try with a 78 rpm. We'd have to do it over and over, just trying to get the edits right, and we'd be laughing at each other the whole time because, whenever one of us would get it right, the other would do something wrong. Oh, and we had no mute button. We had a pot—a fader—on each turntable, so one would go down and one would go up. Sometimes it actually worked, but 99 percent of the time it didn't. We'd end up having to scrap a lot of discs, which made our boss very unhappy.

Things are so convenient today. It's great, but it's also kind of sad that no one has the opportunity to do those kinds of crazy things we had to do. It was difficult, but it was exciting, and it was also a lot of fun.

THE MUSIC

My first break at Apex was the surprise Mercer Ellington session I already told you about. The fact that I pulled it off that day gave me a lot of confidence. It gave other people confidence in me as well, and I began working on bigger sessions.

My first hit at Apex was an R&B record, what was called a "race" record in those days. It was by the Clovers, their first recording for Atlantic Records, and the A-side was called "Don't You Know I Love You?" It was written by Ahmet Ertegun, one of the founders of Atlantic Records, and it was backed by a version of the standard, "Skylark,"[4]

My first hit, "Don't You Know I Love You,"
recorded in 1950.

What happened was, Herb Abrahamson was the producer on the session. Herb had been a dental student who, along with Ahmet, became one of the original partners at Atlantic Records. Herb knew me, and one Saturday he called at the last minute to ask if the studio was available. It was, and he came over with the Clovers. We recorded the two sides in a couple of hours, and "Don't You Know I Love You" became a top ten R&B hit that was on the charts for five months. I had worked on an official hit!

Other recordings I did at the time for Atlantic were a solo record with

Clyde McPhatter, lead singer with the Coasters, and an album of all George Gershwin tunes with singer Chris Connor and the Modern Jazz Quartet.

I also worked with Bobby Shad, a producer who, in 1948, had started a label called Sittin' in With. Bobby was working with Tommy Dowd, recording a lot of great blues and jazz artists and some rock and roll, too. When Tommy was booked, Bobby started using me; I remember in particular doing sessions for Lightnin' Hopkins and Peppermint Harris.

Sales of records were exploding after the war, and a lot of people were getting into the business. It was pretty wild. I remember a producer who'd come in and put his .32 automatic pistol on the producer's desk. The musicians would each get paid something like fifteen dollars in cash after they played the session. I guess the pistol was there just in case somebody tried to take the money away from him. But it definitely scared the hell out of me to see that gun sitting there.

In those days, making records was an all-cash business. I saw that demonstrated with Lightnin' Hopkins. He'd get paid one hundred bucks, he'd play a song, and then he'd stop. He wouldn't do another song until they paid him another hundred bucks. I'm guessing Lightnin' never got paid any royalties, just the hundred dollars cash per song. That's just how it was done.

There were a lot of Mob-connected guys in the music business at the time and they pretty much did things any way they wanted to. A favorite joke at the time was about an artist who went to see record company owner Morris Levy, complaining, "Hey, Morris, I haven't gotten my royalty yet." And Morris said, "You want royalty? Go to England!"

Back then, the people running the companies weren't just executives, they were the people who actually made the records. They knew how the process worked, and it was common practice that they would bootleg their own records. They'd just press up extra records on the side, make photographs of the labels, and print new labels from the photographs, putting in different ID numbers. Then they'd sell them off the loading dock, twenty-five or however many records to a box for as much money they could get. Since it was all done with cash, not only did they avoid paying taxes, they didn't pay the publishers or the artists, either. A lot of people did that kind of stuff then.

Things being free and easy like that then also meant we got to do some really fun things. One I especially liked was that we could get our recordings played right away. I'd have a session with, say, Peppermint Harris and Bobby Shad. We'd cut it on a sixteen-inch transcription disc. Then we'd make a 78 rpm copy on a 10-inch acetate, get in the car with it, and drive up to WHOM radio in Harlem, for the *Willie and Ray Show*, where Willie "the Mayor of Harlem" Bryant and Ray Carroll—who were the first ever multiracial cohosts of a musical radio program—were the top disc jockeys of the day. I don't know if money changed hands or not, but we'd get back in the car and, on the return trip to the studio, we'd get to hear what the song sounded like over the air. That was the coolest.

FULTON RECORDING STUDIO

I spent only a year and a half at Apex with Tom Dowd before the studio went bankrupt and closed. Tommy moved on to a place called Fulton Recording Studio, and I went to a studio called Nola. I worked at Nola, which was a combination of recording and rehearsal studios, for about a year and then I got a call from Tommy. Fulton was looking for another engineer and he'd recommended me. I went over, he introduced me to the owner, and I got the job—for a lot more money than I was getting at Nola. So, Tommy and I were reunited. Later, Fulton was bought by Coastal Recording and the name was changed to Coastal. I stayed at that studio until I left for California in 1958.

Fulton was at 80 West Fortieth Street. It was doing a lot of work for Tico Records, projects with popular Latin musicians like Tito Rodriguez, Tito Puente, and Machito. Cab Calloway worked there as well. It was a big room with high ceilings, and it was believed to have previously been Randolph Hearst's penthouse apartment, which he shared with his mistress Marion Davies, the famous actress, hostess, and philanthropist. Fulton just had one studio, but it was a really good one. Like Abbey Road Studio Two, the control room was above the recording room and you had to go down a flight of stairs to get to the studio. Something really cool about Fulton was that it had a live echo chamber, a little room that Tommy and I would shellac all the time to keep it sounding good. There were no artificial reverbs then, so that little chamber was a big deal to us.

THE ORCHESTRAS

It was at Fulton that I got my first experience recording an orchestra. At Apex, we didn't have enough space to do the kind of setup big orchestras required. Even big bands were tough to fit in at Apex. But when I got to Fulton, we could do everything, and we did.

Engineer Bob Doherty, who was also on staff at Fulton, had learned to record at radio station WOR in New York, where all the music was live. He was the nicest guy you'd ever want to meet, and also one of the best orchestra engineers around. I learned a lot from him: what microphones to use and where to put them, and also about how to work with the orchestra musicians. Again, I mostly learned by watching what he did.

At Fulton, we were all engineers in our own right, but if you weren't busy doing something else, you'd help the other engineers set up their sessions. Often, we'd all pitch in to set up for the orchestras. The consoles were still very small then; I think the most inputs we had was eighteen, so we still weren't using a lot of microphones.

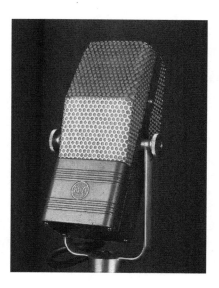

RCA 44 ribbon microphones. *(Photograph by Bill Gibson)*

We didn't have a lot of inputs in the console, but we did have a lot of different mics to choose from. We had RCA 44 and 77-DX ribbon mics. We

RCA 77-DX ribbon microphones.
(*Photograph by Bill Gibson*)

Western
Electric/
Altec 633A
"Salt Shaker."
(*Photograph
courtesy of Prof.
S. O. Coutant*)

had the Western Electric/Altec 633As, which were dynamic mics. We called them the "Salt Shakers" because they were small cylinders with little holes across the top. There were also tube U 47s designed and built by George Neumann for Telefunken to distribute under their diamond badge logo and an Altec M11A condenser tube microphone system with the funny looking black M21B mic that we'd hang up over the drums. We also had the little Altec "Lipstik" mic, the M20 condenser, that we'd tape inside the bridge of basses, which helped give us some isolation and definition. Bass players would let you do that in those days—today they'd be too afraid you'd mess up their instruments. Back then, they didn't seem to care that much.[5]

That was probably because we were always working so fast. We were usually doing four songs in three hours. You had to learn quickly, especially at Fulton, and you had to move quickly, too. You'd set everything up, and then you'd run upstairs to the control room. If you realized a mic wasn't working, you'd have to hustle back down the stairs from the control room to the studio to change it. And if you decided another mic didn't sound quite right for that particular section or instrument, you'd have to do the same. We definitely stayed in shape going up and down those stairs all the time.

The studio had its own drum kits and we also had percussion instru-

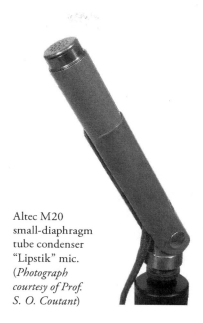

The Altec M11A microphone system featuring the M21B microphone. (*Photograph by Bill Gibson*)

Altec M20 small-diaphragm tube condenser "Lipstik" mic. (*Photograph courtesy of Prof. S. O. Coutant*)

ments—vibes and all kinds of stuff—available. It was actually rare for drummers to bring their own kit, and having the instruments already on hand made setting up faster.

Bob showed me what mics to use and where to put them, but the major secret I learned from him about recording orchestras was to go out into the studio, stand next to the conductor, and listen to what was going on from that perspective. Because you want to capture exactly what the conductors are hearing, and when you're out there with them, you get to hear it like they do. That helps you know what you should be listening for in the control room.

I also learned to not only listen from the conductor's perspective, but also to talk to the conductor and the arranger. If you're getting too much or not enough of some instruments, you can tell them and they'll work with the musicians to help you out.

Other things I learned from Bob were mostly about the art of setup. He and the other engineers had figured out the best-sounding spots in the room for each section, and he showed me where in the room to put the strings, and all of the other instruments, too. In general, we'd set up the orchestras the same way every time. The same thing with the big bands; we'd set them all up the same way, no matter who the bandleader was. Because, pretty much, the engineers had figured out what sounded good where in the room. Because of that, once the players and their instruments set up, it was just a matter of getting the right blend.

Watching Bob, I also learned about demeanor. He was always very relaxed and in control. On his sessions, no one worried about anything and there was no stress. He always seemed to know exactly what he was doing. He was also a patient, kind, nice guy. When you're dealing with that many people in a room, your demeanor makes a big difference.

As it turned out, Bob decided before I did that I was ready to do a big orchestra date by myself. A session for a Gillette razor commercial with about fifty musicians was scheduled, and normally Bob would have been the engineer to do the date. But he pulled me aside and said, "You're going to have to engineer this one, Al. My son has something important happening at his school and I have to be there for it."

I'd watched him do it many times by then, but orchestras were still intimidating to me so my response was, "No, no, no! I have a fear of French horns. They point in the wrong direction and I don't understand how they work." That just made him laugh. He said, "Al, French horns don't bite." Then he and I sat down together, and he walked me through what I'd have to do, showing me where to set things up and what mics to use.

Of course, I did the date, even though I was so nervous during the session that when I walked up to the console, I kept my hands in my pockets so that no one would see how much they were shaking. And when I sat down, I took them out of my pockets and grabbed onto the big rotary faders, so they'd stay steady and people wouldn't notice the shaking.

Once again, I got through it. When it was done, as frightened as I'd been, I realized that I'd also really enjoyed it. It became one of my very favorite things to do. The bigger the orchestra, the more fun it was—for me, anyway. I loved it.

For me, the more people you have in the studio the easier it actually is to record. Sound-wise, recording sixty-five pieces is a snap. It's much more difficult to record an eight-piece band where all the instruments have their own microphones or direct boxes and each person is playing something different.

With a sixty-five-piece orchestra, you have sections—and generally, really good players. You might have a setup with twenty violins, eight violas, eight cellos, four French horns, eight basses, four trumpets, four trombones, and four woodwinds, plus maybe a harp, chimes, and percussion, or maybe a tuba—all of that. You've got multiple sections, plus a conductor out there in front of the musicians who can help you with balances—a little more of this or that within the sections. Because of the large number of instruments in the sections, you get the full weight and blend of the sound.

With an eight-piece band, you've got separate instruments playing separate parts. You can't just say, "I want a little less trumpet or drums." It's much more up to you, as the engineer, to take care of how it sounds. Believe me, once everything is set up, in place, and working, the orchestra is easier. There's nothing that sounds like all of those pieces going off together in an orchestra. Even with just the string section, when you open up the microphones with all of the basses, cellos, violas and violins, it sounds wonderful. And truthfully, it's all captured with the overhead microphones. With a full orchestra of good players all in a room together, it's really magnificent.

I worked with Neil Young on his 2014 album *Storytone*. We did seven songs with orchestra and three with big bands, and we did it like in the old days, with everything live. Some of the sessions had one hundred pieces: a sixty-five-person orchestra and thirty-five-voice choir on the big soundstage on the Sony Pictures lot in Culver City. We had two days with the orchestra at Sony and one day with the big band at East West Studios in Hollywood. No headphones, no after-the-fact tuning, no editing; everyone just straight to 2-track. Neil stood out there with the rhythm section and the orchestra, singing and playing harmonica in the studio with all the musicians. It was wonderful.

I still love recording orchestras; it really is my favorite thing these days. Of course, it's how I learned because, back in the day, that was the way we all recorded. Everything was live—that's just the way it was. And when you do that, part of what's so great is that what you're hearing while you're recording is what you're going to get in the final product.

I'm not really in favor of overdubbing everyone. When I learned, you had to capture it all in the moment. You had to really be on your toes and know what you were doing, but it was also a lot of fun—more than overdubbing guitars or synthesizers for hours at a time.

Overdubbing is the way records are made today, so you do your job and get it done. But it just isn't quite as much fun. When you're working with musicians, they play off one another. Everybody is moving and playing and learning from one another. Then everyone locks up together, and it's a great feeling to be a part of that.

Of course, to record a lot of musicians live, you have to make sure everything is right. You've got to get the balances and be on top of all the cues. With orchestras and big bands, we always have someone following the score. They'll call out to me, "Al, they're going to mutes in two bars," so I'll be ready to push the trumpets up at that point. There's really nothing like it. What's sad now is that there are only a few people left who know how to do those big dates, and people have almost nowhere to go to learn. I hope this book helps with that.

See Appendix B for a diagram of the Neil Young *Storytone* sessions, showing the placement of the musicians in the studio and the microphones that were used to record them.

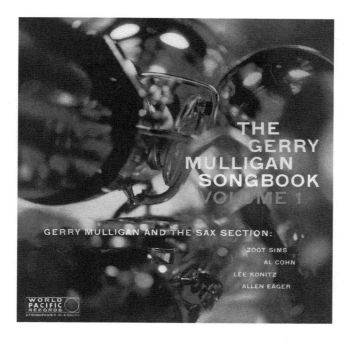

OTHER SESSIONS AT FULTON

At Fulton, I also worked a lot for the World Pacific and Pacific Jazz labels that were founded by producer Dick Bock and drummer Roy Harte. I did Gerry Mulligan's *Reunion* album with Chet Baker. It was a quartet: bass, drums, sax, and Chet, of course, on trumpet. For that one, I remember that we actually did two different mic setups for mono and stereo. For the mono, there were four mics, one each on the trumpet, the sax, the drums, and the bass. The stereo was recorded separately to a different 2-track machine with only two mics, set up high to cover the whole band. This was in 1957. I was still a baby![6]

I also did *The Gerry Mulligan Songbook*, which was performed by an octet with five saxophones. That was an incredible seven song album, recorded with all of the saxophones around one microphone. Gerry was on baritone sax, which he was known for, with Lee Konitz on alto, Allen Eager and Zoot Sims on tenor and alto, and Al Cohn on tenor and baritone. The rhythm section was guitarist Freddie Green, bassist Henry Grimes, and drummer Dave Bailey. Another standout from around that time for me was the album called

The Street Swingers that I did with valve trombone player Bobby Brookmeyer and the fabulous guitarists Jim Hall and Jimmy Raney.

Remember, back then everything was still released in mono. I did a lot of the World Pacific and Pacific Jazz recordings in both mono and stereo, but we used separate setups for each, with different mics and recorders for the stereo.

Sometimes we'd just use two mics over the band for stereo and go direct from the mics into the stereo machine, which was usually a small tape machine, not a big Ampex, without going through the board.

We'd go back and forth listening to the outputs of both machines while we were recording to make sure the stereo was okay. But basically, the stereo version was just left alone while the music was being recorded. It was what it was, because we were still so much more concerned with getting the mono right.

Stereo was still a stepsister at the time. It hadn't become a big thing because people didn't yet have stereo playback systems in their home. We knew it was coming—or at least the record company guys in charge of the sessions kept telling us it was coming! We were recording a lot of great artists at the time, and all of the labels wanted to ensure they had their artists covered for stereo. But for a very long time, mono remained the important thing. When the records were released, the stereo recordings were just put into the label vaults to be ready for when stereo caught on.

There were, however, some very experimental stereo recordings being made at that time, and when I got to Los Angeles, I worked on one of them with engineer John Norman at RCA. It was for Juan García Esquivel, who was an innovator known for making eccentric pop that was sometimes called space-age music. The recording I worked on with Esquivel was the sequel to his *Other Worlds, Other Sounds*, which had been engineered by Ralph Valentine. The one I did was called *More Other Worlds, Other Sounds*.

We recorded, as Esquivel liked to do, simultaneously in two studios; half of the band was in Studio A and half was in Studio B, with John engineering in one studio and me in the other. Something would happen in one room and then something else in the other, with all sorts of spinning sounds and crazy effects. There were no video cameras in those days, so John and I couldn't see what was going on in each other's studio. It was quite a mal de mer, as we called it, meaning it kind of made you seasick to listen to it. But it was true stereo, and it was groundbreaking.

4

THE WEST COAST CALLS:
LOS ANGELES IN THE SIXTIES AND SEVENTIES

WHILE I WAS working at Fulton, producer Dick Bock would often come to New York to use me on his dates. Finally, at one point he asked me, "Why don't you move to California? Then I wouldn't have to travel all this way to record." I told him, "Get me a job out there and I'll come." About three weeks later, Dick called and said that there was an opening at a studio in Los Angeles and its management was interested in hiring me. It was 1958, and the studio was Radio Recorders. I got the job, moved to California, and went right to work.

STAFF ENGINEER: RADIO RECORDERS AND RCA

Radio Recorders was located at 7000 Santa Monica Boulevard at the corner of Orange Drive. It had opened sometime in the early 1940s, and it had five studios that were mostly used for radio shows. Studio B was the largest studio, and the one that was most often used for music recording sessions. Most of the major labels used Radio Recorders' studios because they didn't yet have their own recording facilities on the West Coast. RCA in particular made it its home base for recording. In the late 1950s, Elvis Presley had recorded his hits "Jailhouse Rock," "All Shook Up," and "Party Doll" there, and it was considered by many people to be the best recording facility in Los Angeles.

It was a great studio to work in, and I was glad I'd made the move. When I first came to work there, I became known for having what was being called a "New York–style" sound and a lot of people liked it. I think part of what they were hearing came about because, at that time in New

York, we were using a lot of tube microphones, especially U 47s. Back then, you could buy a U 47, made by Telefunken/Neumann, for three hundred bucks. For the time, that certainly wasn't cheap, but it wasn't anywhere near as expensive as they are today. The tube microphone distributors were all based in New York then, so maybe that's why they were more common in New York than Los Angeles; the distributors were bringing them by the studio all the time and we got to try them.

Whatever the reason, we used them a lot in New York, and when I first came out to Los Angeles and put a U 47 on upright bass, people were surprised. Nobody else that I saw was doing that—at least at Radio Recorders. They were using ribbons and other kinds of mics, but there weren't a lot of tube mics around. So, that's where my "sound" came in—the Al Schmitt sound was really the New York sound, and the New York sound in large part came from the use of tube mics.

At Radio Recorders, producers were making a lot of records for big jazz artists, and they were recording them as quickly as possible so they could save money and sell them at a lower price. Dave Pell was one of those producers. He liked my work, and I started doing a lot of dates for him. Also, a lot of the guys I'd worked with in New York asked for me whenever they came out to California.

The sessions I was doing were fun, and there were a lot of Hollywood people around. I did an album with the great actress Maureen O'Hara, and still remember that I got a kiss on the cheek from her. And Duke, John Wayne, her good friend who had made many movies with her, would come by to visit. Duke was truly huge—bigger than life.

I was also working a lot with Shorty Rogers, who was one of the founders of the musical style called West Coast jazz. Don't ask me to tell you what that was, though. I've worked on a lot of jazz records and with a lot of jazz musicians, but I truly don't know what the difference was between West Coast and East Coast jazz. And I think if you look it up, you'll see that I'm not the only one to say so. I guess the players in New York may have thought they were hipper, but it wasn't something that really mattered to the musicians. The only real difference I can see is where the players lived! For the musicians, there was no East Coast and West Coast. It was just jazz.[1]

Shorty played trumpet and was a great arranger, bandleader, and composer as well. He had a pseudonym he used when he did rock and roll records; he called himself Boots Brown for those sessions. They were listed as "by Boots Brown and His Blockbusters." Those were really fun records. Shorty did unusual things on them, like putting a kazoo in the bell of a trumpet—so it acted as a mute but also made a buzzing sound like a kazoo. He was a serious player, but he also liked to have fun. I worked with Shorty on music for one of the Tarzan movies; the cover of the album had Tarzan holding Shorty in his arms.

During that time, I also did a record, *Ray Charles and Betty Carter*, that's still one of my favorites. It should be on your "must-listen" list. Marty Paich did the arrangements. It was Ray at the piano singing into a U 47, with Betty standing next to him at another U 47, so that she could put her hand on his shoulder while they recorded. They were in the room with strings and a choir—the Johnny Mann Singers—and a seated horn section with saxes, trombones, and trumpets. We didn't have a solo mic; the sax soloist stayed where he was seated, and when it came time for his solos, he just stood up and leaned into the mic.

See Appendix B for a diagram of the *Ray Charles and Betty Carter* sessions.

That was another album made in three sessions; nine hours total, live to both mono and 2-track for stereo. We were still hardly ever listening to the stereo; we just pulled everything we had panned in the center for the stereo mix down 3 dB (decibels) in the stereo feed, which reduced their level by half. We had to do that, because all of the same mics that went to the mono mix were also going to the stereo feed. If they'd been panned to the center, they would have been sent equally to both sides of the stereo mix and it would have made everything panned to the center louder than it should have been.

It was around that time that I had a very big record, a huge hit for Connie Francis called "My Happiness," that she did with David Rose (the composer of "The Stripper") and his orchestra. After that I was, literally, working all the time. Then, only a little more than a year after I'd moved from New York, my big Los Angeles break came.

Bones Howe was a terrific engineer and producer who also worked at Radio Recorders. We were both young up-and-comers and we became very good friends. At one point, Bones was working with Henry Mancini on a project where Henry was the artist. I'd previously worked with Henry in his role as an arranger; that's primarily what he was first known for. He was a really laid-back guy, very polite, and a great orchestrator. I still remember how he looked the first time I saw him in the studio, up on the conductor stand, smoking his pipe, totally relaxed and very, very cool.

What happened was, Bones was scheduled to work with Henry and, for these particular dates, Simon "Sy" Rady, who'd worked a lot with Bing Crosby and Judy Garland, was producing. I have no idea what went on, but I guess Bones and Sy somehow got into a disagreement. What caused it, I never found out, but Sy asked for me to work on the sessions instead. That meant Bones had done the first half of the album and I ended up doing the second half. Which turned out to be a very big deal, because the project was *The Music from Peter Gunn* album, and it became a huge hit.[2]

Working with Hank was great, and *Peter Gunn* made him famous. It just exploded. RCA had no idea what was going on; the record was so big that they didn't have enough album covers. They had plenty of pressings, but no jackets. They put the discs in plain white covers and sold them with a little slip of paper and a note that let you come back in a couple of weeks and get the jackets. That's how big it was.

The people at RCA liked my work on that album, and from then on I was pretty much their guy. I began doing almost all of the RCA work at Radio Recorders with Shorty and also Dick Pierce—who was producing so many big acts at the time, like Lena Horne, Tony Martin, Ray Peterson and Jesse Belvin. And then, I also started doing all the Mancini projects and Dick was the producer on most of those, too.

Hank was one of the dearest people, just a really good guy, but he had a wicked sense of humor. When I was first working with him and we were doing big orchestra dates, I'd be working away with all the faders up on the board. He'd come in with his big pages of score, and put them down right on top of the console so that he pushed all the faders up to the top. I'd tell him not to do that, and he'd do it again anyway. He'd just look at me and smile. Finally, I got smart: I'd mark the faders before he came in. That way, he could do what he wanted, and after he left, I could put the faders back where I'd had them.

He wasn't being mean, it was just his little joke. I was in charge of the sound; he was in charge of making the hits, and he wanted to see how fast I could get things back together when he messed them up for me. After that, I called him "Hitmaker" and he called me "Soundmaker," and he'd become "Hank" to me, not Henry.

The next thing I did with Hank was *More Music from Peter Gunn*. By that time, I'd left Radio Recorders and was working on staff for RCA. They had so much going on that they'd decided to build their own studios on Sunset and Vine in Hollywood, and I was the first engineer they hired. That was another big break for me, and again I was working all the time. Too much, but that's just the way it was.

There were two studios at RCA and the bigger room was the best studio I'd ever worked in. The smaller one was great, too, and it wasn't really small—you could put a big band in there with no trouble at all.

The sessions at RCA with Hank were particularly wonderful. In 1961, we did the soundtrack for *Breakfast at Tiffany's* and "Moon River," the single. It was in the big studio at RCA, and a lot of people from the movie showed up for the session, which was all done live, with a choir of twelve or so people, including Hank's wife, and a huge string section and woodwinds. I got my first Grammy nomination that year when *Breakfast at Tiffany's* was nominated for Best Engineered Recording. I lost, though, because that year the award went to the engineer who had done Judy Garland's live album, *Judy at Carnegie Hall*.

But the following year, 1962, I did *Hatari!* with Hank. It also got nominated for Best Engineered Recording, and that year, I won. It was my first Grammy Award, and also probably the most difficult record I've done in my life.

The score for *Hatari!* was immensely complicated, and, like most of Hank's recordings then, all done live—everything at the same time. *Hatari!* though, was truly an engineer's nightmare. Not only was there no overdubbing in those days, there were no click tracks, and there were no isolation booths. Everybody had to see one another, and they also all had to see Hank, because he was conducting. Everything had to be done at one time in one big room. I recall John Williams, who went on to become such a hugely famous film composer, played piano on some of the album. We called him Johnny Williams back then.

There's a seven-minute cut on the album called "The Sounds of Hatari," and you really need to listen to it. It's the opening cut, and it is still probably the most difficult recording I've done in my life. There were five percussionists across the back of the room playing all kinds of strange instruments, including the great drummer Shelly Manne playing kalimba—the African thumb piano. There was a log bass, a very low-sounding instrument that was an actual hollowed-out tree trunk played with mallets. There were also what we called the "beans," huge pods with dried beans inside that were used as giant shakers. These were all authentic instruments that Hank had brought back from Tanganyika in Africa where they were shooting the film. We also had a bunch of other drums, along with strings, French horns, woodwinds, trombones, marimba, vibes, and five guys sitting around two Neumann M 49s set in bidirectional, playing bass flutes. Oh, and a tack piano, an upright with tacks placed on the felt hammers to give it a more percussive sound. You always mike tack pianos from the back and I remember using two RCA 77-DXs on it.

Try to get separation between the instruments with all that going on! There were microphones everywhere. Was it tough? Yes. That's why I won the Grammy. I think all the engineers who voted for me had understood my challenges when they heard the record. They knew how difficult it was.

We did the whole album in mono and 2-track—at the same time, of course. But, as usual, we were just listening to the mono. And even now, if you listen to it, you'll most likely be hearing it in mono. That's how it was released.

I actually didn't think the album would win a Grammy because it wasn't as popular as some other recordings made that year. The hit off the *Hatari!* album was "Baby Elephant Walk," which seemed to be a little simpler orchestration-wise than the rest of the album. But even on "Walk," there's a calliope, then all of a sudden brass and French horns came in. Nothing on the *Hatari* album was simple.

After *Hatari!*, we did *Charade, Two for the Road, Experiment in Terror, The Blues in the Beat, Mr. Lucky*, and *Mr. Lucky Goes Latin*. Most were soundtracks but not all. Each, however, was unique.

How we did those complicated dates was, I'd find out what we were doing the day of the session, then Hank and I would sit down to figure it out together. We'd talk about how, as the conductor, he'd like it set up, and I'd decide what microphones to use.

After a while at RCA, the assistants I worked with knew how I liked things, which helped a lot. By then, I was doing three sessions a day, so when I'd finish my second date of the day, which ran two to five p.m., I'd have three hours before Hank's eight p.m. session. Just enough time to eat, relax a little bit, and still be back in the studio to make sure everything was set up correctly.

I don't read music, but I can follow a score. I learned how to do that when I was working for Hank. With so much happening all at once, I had to learn where the violins played, where the organ solo was—all of that— and be ready for them. I had to be able to count the bars and see exactly what was going to be happening where and when. These days, I don't have to read scores and count bars anymore; my assistants do it. They call out cues for me: "The trumpets are on mutes; the trumpets are open; a big tutti is coming." They follow the score along and let me know what they see coming up.

Although I was also working with a lot of other artists, Hank was such a big client, and I was working with him so much, that when RCA was going to promote me to producer, he wouldn't let them do it until I got someone to take my place. Which I did. There was an engineer at Radio Recorders named Jim Malloy. I liked Jim and thought he had a lot of talent, so I brought him over to RCA as an engineer and worked with him on the Mancini dates until he could do them on his own. Jim ended up recording "The Pink Panther Theme" and eventually went on to become a very successful producer in Nashville. With Jim in place working the Mancini sessions, I was able to move up and become an RCA staff producer.

STAFF PRODUCER: RCA

As an engineer at RCA, I was in demand, almost always doing those three dates a day, and making good money. Each date was three hours and we were always trying to get four songs done in a date. The sessions were nine a.m. to noon, two to five p.m. and eight to eleven p.m. I'd do that six days a week, generally with a different artist for each session. One day it could be Ike and Tina Turner, the Ventures, and Sam Cooke. The next day it could be Henry Mancini, Ray Charles with Betty Carter, and Rosemary Clooney.

I'd do a country record with Bobby Bare, and right after that I'd record a big band with Billy May and Billy Eckstine. Then that night, I'd be doing something with singer Gloria Lynne. One right after the other, with just a couple of hours between them to clear the room, have our meal break, then reset for the next session. We also did all the teardown and setup ourselves. There were assistants at RCA, but no setup people. It was just the engineer and the assistant to do everything.

As an engineer, I was working so much and so hard that all sorts of producers started hearing about me and requesting to have me on their sessions. But some of those producers, instead of working with the musicians, would spend most of their three-hour session on the phone. Some of them just weren't paying attention, and some of them really didn't know what they were doing. They couldn't tell if there were bad notes or if something wasn't in tune. It was an open secret, and it became a joke with the players, "We're on the honor system here, guys. If you make a mistake, raise your hand."

Still, whether they were paying attention or not, or knew what they were doing or not, the producers got all the glory. For example, on the session I did with Connie Francis and arranger David Rose, the producer was there for the first two songs, because those were the songs that he was interested in. When we were done with those two songs, he left.

The third song was "My Happiness," and we did it without him. We recorded it, and then we decided to double the voice. We were still just mono on this date, so we had to bring in another tape machine to be able to double track. Connie sang along to the original recording, and we recorded to the second machine, so the master was a copy except for the doubled voice. It was difficult, but we did it, and it worked. Connie was very pleased with our extra efforts and she said to me, "Al, if this record goes to number one, you're going to walk out of the studio door and find a brand-new car sitting out there for you."

Well, "My Happiness" went to number one for ten weeks, and every time I opened the studio door and looked out, I'd see that there was no car.

You can tell what kind of frame of mind I was getting into at that time from this crazy story I remember. There was a producer who wanted to book the RCA studio for a project, but he said he would only work with me. I'd never heard of him, and I kept telling my boss, Charlie Pruzansky, that I couldn't do it. I'd say, "I'm so busy, I don't have time for this guy, Charlie. Plus, I don't know even know who he is. Can't I please just get a little time off instead? I really need some time off." But the guy persisted, and finally Charlie got tired of dealing with him and said, "This guy is driving us nuts. You have to do the date."

So, okay, I agreed to do it. My assistant at the time was Dave Hassinger. Dave became a great engineer in his own right, but at that point I was breaking him in and he hadn't done any real record dates yet. Before the session, I sent him to the Army Navy Store on Santa Monica Boulevard, where he found an old hearing aid box from the 1940s. You can imagine what that looked like. It was pretty frightening, a metal box that hung over your chest with a speaker in it. I put it on, and when the guy showed up for the date I went up to him and said, "Hi, I'm Al Schmitt." Meanwhile, I kept knocking the box with my fist because the speaker was cutting out. The look on the client's face was priceless; it only lasted a minute, but it was worth it.

He turned snow white and Dave and I almost fell on the floor laughing. When the client realized it was a joke, he was pretty cool. But to this day it makes me laugh to recall the expression on his face when I pretended I couldn't hear what he was saying. Here he was finally coming to do his big recording date. He'd succeeded in getting the great Al Schmitt to do his session, and, as it turned out, the great Al Schmitt, apparently, was deaf.

It was pretty clear that I thought I'd had enough of engineering, and that I wanted to be promoted to staff producer. I was ready, and I got my wish. But there were union rules in those days about who did what. So, for four years, from 1962 to 1966, I couldn't touch the board. And there were other things I hadn't really foreseen when I'd decided I wanted to be a producer.

In those days, there were no points—percentages—for producers, and there was no such thing as an independent producer. Even the top producers, like the Beatles producer George Martin, and Dick Pierce, who produced the Mancini records, were all staff producers, just like what I'd become at RCA. They got salaries and a bonus. And as it turned out, I soon discovered that I'd actually made more money as an engineer than as a producer.

As a producer, I was making $17,500 a year and I could make a bonus of $5,000. I made the bonus every year, because I was working with popular artists like Sam Cooke and Eddie Fisher all the time and their records did very well.

I'd always worked hard as a staff engineer, generally those three sessions a day. But it was different as a producer. There was much more to do than just the recording sessions, and the workload really was too much.

I love my work, so for me to say that is a lot. But it's true. I was working with Eddie Fisher in the afternoon from two to five, then I'd go to my office on the second floor and meditate for an hour—Paul Horn, who was one of my artists, had gotten me into Transcendental Meditation. Then the Jefferson Airplane sessions started at eight at night. We were doing *After Bathing at Baxter's*, which was like a zoo. They would come riding into the studio on motorcycles, and they were getting high all the time. They had a nitrous oxide tank set up in the studio, they'd be rolling joints all night, and there was a lot of cocaine.

Plus, Owsley was there with acid. There were no three-hour sessions for the Airplane. Since they were the artists, and played all the instruments, and because they were so successful, they were able to do whatever they wanted. We'd be in the studio till four in the morning. Then, I'd go home and get a few hours of sleep until it was time to get up and go back to my office, where I had all sorts of other things to get done before my afternoon Eddie Fisher session began.[3]

At the time, as a producer, I was responsible for eleven artists: Sam Cooke, Eddie Fisher, Gail Garnett, Paul Horn, Jefferson Airplane, the Limelighters, Ann-Margret, Hugo Montenegro, Bobby Pickett, a group called the Womenfolk, and Glenn Yarbrough. That was an era when not many artists wrote songs, so, in addition to doing budgets, scheduling, and being in the studio with the artists, I also had to spend a lot of time looking for songs. Every Monday, I'd try to keep time clear for meetings with publishers.

We were doing complete albums in twelve to fifteen hours; for many artists, there was no real mixing. With Ann-Margret, for example, I often did four songs in three hours. Some days we did two three-hour sessions, so it didn't take long to have a full album with twelve songs. It wasn't like today, where an album generally takes weeks, if not longer. With the exception of the Airplane, once we began recording, it took basically two days to make an album. But it was nonstop: sit with the arranger, get that done, go over the song keys with the artists, put together schedules, work on contracts. All that took a lot of time, and then I'd be in the studio with the artists.

Finally, one day, I'd had enough. Ernie Altschuler was my boss at the time. He was the head of A&R at RCA, and his claim to fame was that he'd recorded Tony Bennett's "I Left My Heart in San Francisco." I called Ernie on the phone and said, "I can't do this any longer. I'm working sixteen hours a day, then I go home, get a couple of hours of sleep, and have to come right back and do budgets and everything else. I can't continue doing this."

His reply was, "Why not? Truck drivers do it." I couldn't believe that was his response, and I said, "Ernie, really, truck drivers? He said, "Yeah."

My answer to that was immediate. I didn't even think about it. I said,

"Do yourself a favor then and get a couple of truck drivers. I quit." The next morning, I gave my secretary my two-week notice and left.

GOING INDEPENDENT

That was 1967. I'd left my job and I didn't know what I was going to do next. But, as it turned out, I was only home for a couple of weeks when I got a call from Jefferson Airplane. Now remember, I was making $22,500 with my bonus, and I'd left my job at RCA in the middle of making the Airplane's record. They called and said, "Al, they tried to give us somebody else on staff at RCA to work with. But there's nobody there that we want, and they've agreed to let us bring in an outside producer. They'll give the producer points. Would you do it?"

I said, "Absolutely. Sure!" I went back in with them and finished *After Bathing at Baxter's*, and, to my surprise, my first royalty check for the record was for fifty grand. I'd been doing eleven artists at RCA for $22,500, and now I'd done one record for one band for a lot more money. I decided I'd made the right decision. And I had. Over the next four years, I stayed busy producing records, including several more for the Airplane and their spinoff duo Hot Tuna, which was made up of guitarist Jorma Kaukonen and bass player Jack Casady.

Of course, working with the Airplane was a story unto itself. We'll talk more about that later.

5

LIKE RIDING A BIKE

BUT THEN, I think I got really lucky because I got back into engineering.

I had gotten to know Tommy LiPuma when he was working for a song publisher and he would come by my office at RCA to pitch songs. We hit it off, became great friends, and used to hang out together all the time. In 1971, Tommy was producing a record for Dave Mason, the singer, songwriter, and guitarist who had been a founder of the band Traffic. Bruce Botnick was engineering most of the album. But Bruce had a prior commitment with the Doors, and when he wasn't available to mix the Dave Mason record, Tommy asked me if I would do it. The problem was, though, since I'd become a producer, I hadn't done any engineering or mixing. It had been more than four years, and it felt like such a long time away from engineering that I didn't have confidence in my ability to get back behind the board. So, I told Tommy I didn't know if I'd really be capable of doing the job.

He said, "Al, it's like riding a bike."

BACK TO ENGINEERING

I thought about what Tommy said, and then we made a pact: if I felt like I wasn't doing well, or he thought it wasn't going right, we had to tell each other, no hard feelings, and he'd get someone else to do the mixes. Tommy agreed, we started, and as I got into mixing that record, I began to realize how much I missed engineering and how much I loved recording and mixing. After all, it was the reason I originally got into the music business. What I loved best about the business in the first place was capturing the sound.

The album was *Alone Together*, Dave's debut as a solo artist. It turned out to be a great record, with a hit called "Only You Know and I Know," and the great "Shouldn't Have Took More Than You Gave." It felt so good to work on it. I was thrilled with the way it came out, and I was thrilled that I was able to do it.

After that, I got a call from Jackson Browne, and I did *Everyman* with him as the engineer. We got along so well that we coproduced his next album, *Late for the Sky*. Then, I got a call from Neil Young, and I engineered and coproduced *On the Beach*. Doing that record with Neil was my first real experience with how artists can get attached to rough mixes. When we were finished and I was ready to mix, Neil told me that we didn't need mixes. He liked what we'd already done.

My style of working is that I'm already thinking about mixing when I'm recording, but for that record I was definitely also planning on having time just to mix. When Neil said no, I begged him. I said, "Neil, I'll do it for free!" When he still wouldn't agree, I said, "I'll pay for the studio time!" But his answer didn't change. It was still no, and he released the album with the rough mixes on it.

That was forty years ago, and we laugh about it now. My friend Niko Bolas works with Neil a lot, and Neil always tells him, "Say hello to Al, and ask him if he still wants to remix *On the Beach*." And my answer is still, always, yes!

As an independent I was busy, both producing and engineering. But then, very naturally, it started to happen that I was doing mostly engineering.

I think there are two reasons for that. One was artistic. For me, it's similar to how a painter has a brush in his or her hand. At that time, as a producer, you were directing the sound, but you didn't have the brush in your hand. The engineer had the actual brush. Some people say it's like being a chef, where you start with the right ingredients, and if you add a little of this and a little of that, you get a great meal. It's the same with mixing. A little of this bass, a little bit of drums, a touch of guitar. Then you add a pinch of piano in there and you make a great record.

That's how I felt about it. I liked that creative feeling and the art of it. The other reason was practical. Technically, I wanted to be physically hands on. I couldn't do that when I was producing because, in those days, there were strict union rules about who did what job. RCA was union, so every time I'd reach over to do something myself, someone would complain to management and I'd get called up on the carpet. I wasn't supposed to touch any of the equipment, and having to explain to someone else how I wanted the bass to sound was sometimes very frustrating.

Fortunately, I was lucky in the engineers I got to work with. For example, my brother Richy Schmitt, as I've mentioned, was also an engineer, and a really good one. I had helped get him on staff at RCA and I often got to work with him when I was producing. Hank Cicalo is another great engineer I got to work with a lot. There were so many great engineers at RCA, and some of them—if there was nobody else around to see—would let me get hands on and make adjustments. But that wasn't the norm, and there were occasions when by the time I told someone what I wanted, it was too late. If I'd been the engineer, I could have just reached over and done it myself. That's the position I wanted to be in, and that's how it came about that I went back to engineering.

HOW TO LISTEN

I've been listening seriously to music since I started visiting my uncle's studio when I was seven. So really, how I listen is just part of who I am. It developed over all my years of being in the studio—first, when I was really young, just being there watching and listening to what was going on. Then I was lucky to be an apprentice for a little while, working with Tom Dowd at Apex, and then as an engineer, working in studios with other engineers like Bob Doherty who were really outstanding at their work.

All of those things helped develop my ears. Plus, of course, I've been listening to live musical performances and recordings made by other engineers all my life. Listening to music isn't just my job, it's my passion.

There's really no substitute for all that time spent listening; my ear training came through years of experience. Listening is so much a part of who I am that it's actually kind of difficult for me to verbalize how I listen and what I'm listening for. I think that is probably true of most good engineers who have been around for a while. It's just something that gets ingrained in you. That said, I can think of a few things to say on this topic.

Something important I learned early on was to listen to an overall product. People can often get too locked in on a certain instrument or a specific sound, and they'll end up spending too much time on something that's really just an incidental part of the mix. You really have to take a step back so that you're hearing the whole picture and how everything works together. I probably developed some of that skill when I started out and we were working, by necessity, with so few microphones.

And I'll say it again, when you are recording musicians, leave the control room, go out in the studio where they are playing, and listen. Your job is to capture what they are doing. Listen to make sure there is no distortion, because you want a clean signal. But for the actual sound of the recording, if you can make it sound like what you heard out in the studio, you are on your way.

When you're listening, it's also important to pay attention to the inherent dynamics of the music. What engineers call the "loudness wars" have, for me, made some records unlistenable. The theory behind that is that the recording that sounds the loudest will be the most appealing to listeners. It's not a new theory, but now that there are so many different ways to add compression to create perceived loudness, it's really gotten out of hand.[1]

Often now, when you hear songs on the radio, they've got broadcast compression added to the huge amount of compression that was already put on during mixing and mastering. To me, they sound distorted and really, just plain terrible.

Sometimes also, there is so much midrange equalization (EQ) added, in an attempt to give the songs more presence, that it cuts like a razorblade and hurts my ears.

I don't know why people do this and there's actually an organization I belong to called Turn Me Up! (www.turnmeup.org) that's all about bringing dynamics back to music. You want it louder? Turn it up. The reason we have volume knobs on our playback equipment is so that if you want something louder, you can turn it up. A lot of us who are engineers don't like everything being slammed so hard, and we got together to try to let people know what they're missing when music is overcompressed. A lot of engineers would really like to see more natural dynamics in music, and we believe that recordings don't need to be heavily compressed to be competitive.

You can lose a lot of the feeling and emotion of a song when it's aggressively compressed during mixing and mastering. All that processing also changes the sound, and it is often better musically to just let the song have some room to breathe. Listeners can use the volume knob to make a song louder if they want to. That way, you'll preserve the original dynamics and overall sound of the music, which will most likely have a much stronger emotional impact on the listener.

WHAT I LISTEN ON

At home, I listen on a pair of self-powered model AMS 8A Tannoy speakers that I bought about twelve years ago. I listen to vinyl quite a bit, on an Audio-Technica AT-LP5 turntable. I do think vinyl sounds better and that it generally has a higher quality than you'll find on CDs. I think that's often because there is more care put into cutting vinyl, and that, in general, the people who cut it have great expertise and understanding. They have to be very careful about sibilance and other things like the amount of bass and the overall balance. There's a lot of minutia to mastering vinyl and a lot of detail work. You have to really care about what you're doing.

Of course, with vinyl there's also a psychological factor. There is definitely something different about playing a record for fifteen minutes, then having to get up and turn it over to listen for another fifteen minutes. Plus, there are album art and credits to look at. All those things mean you're probably going to pay more attention to the music in general. It's not just in the background.

Doug Sax, my longtime mastering engineer, was one of the best in the world at cutting vinyl. He's gone now, but there are people who learned from him, and from the other great masters of vinyl cutting. These days, I use Eric Boulanger at the Bakery, in Los Angeles, who worked with Doug at the Mastering Lab. I love Eric's work for both mastering and cutting vinyl. He cut the Diana Krall vinyl on her latest release, *Turn Up the Quiet*, and it sounds amazing.

CHOOSING MICROPHONES

I love microphones and I love trying new ones. To me, they are like works of art—the great old mics, but also a lot of the new ones. Microphone technology today just keeps getting better. In the past, I always used my AKG C12s for overheads on the drums. They were a set, a matched pair that came right from the factory—absolutely gorgeous microphones.

But then I got a pair of Audio-Technica AT5045s, tried them on the drum overheads, and couldn't believe how good and clear they sounded. They're what I always use now for drum overheads. I almost never pull out my $10,000 pair of C12 microphones anymore; I like the new 5045s better, and so do the drummers. We also tried an AT5045 on the great session guitarist Dean Parks. He loved it, and now it's also my "go-to" acoustic guitar mic.

I try new and different microphones all the time because I'm still always trying to make my recordings just a little bit better. For the way I record, microphones are some of the engineer's paintbrushes. They're what I use to get the palette I want for any given recording. If I put a microphone on an acoustic guitar and I'm not getting what I want out of it, I'll change the mic and it's like changing the color.

I'm very lucky, because most of the time I get to use really great microphones. These days I mostly work at Capitol Studios in Los Angeles, and between my own collection and what Capitol has, there's a huge arsenal available to me. For example, on the early projects I did with Diana Krall, I used a Neumann U 67 that belonged to Tommy LiPuma. It's an especially nice one that's been modified by Klaus Heyne of German Masterworks, who has been customizing microphones for twenty-five years or more.

Then, one day, Diana and her band came into Capitol to record a song live, and they were also going to be capturing the recording on video. Visually, they wanted to use the special Neumann U 48 that Capitol owns that's called the "Frank Sinatra" mic. It was used by Sinatra and also by Nat King Cole and Dean Martin, among many others. It's actually one of my go-to mics and I use it a lot.

When I put it out for Diana to use that day for the video, she wasn't thinking about it and she didn't notice at first that it wasn't her usual mic. But when she put her headphones on and started to sing, she heard the difference right away and said, "Al, what's this?" She fell in love with that microphone immediately. Then, of course, I showed her the special box they had

The iconic "Frank Sinatra" mic at Capitol. We generally refer to
it as a U 47, because it looks just like one, but it's actually a
Neumann U 48.

for it that said "Frank Sinatra" on the side, and after that she started using it
all of the time. It has that effect on people.

You can see that I'm blessed in what I have to choose from. After all my
years of experience, I know what to expect from most microphones and if
something doesn't sound right to my ears, I'll either move the mic to see what
that does, or I'll change to a different mic that I expect may sound better.

Certainly, when you have a mic on the kick drum, just moving the mic an
inch can make a difference. The same with acoustic guitar, piano, or almost
any instrument. The sound also depends on the individual situation—the
room, the instrument, the player, even the humidity that day. That's why I
can't tell people exactly where to put their microphones. Every situation is

different, and every engineer's ears are different. There are starting points, and mics that generally work for specific situations, but you can't just rely on that. You have to listen for yourself.

I used to watch engineers put a mic up on something, decide they wanted it to be a little brighter, and add maybe 8 dB of EQ to it. That's very strange to me. Instead, I'll move, or change, the microphone to enhance the sound. To me, unless you're trying for an effect, adding 8 dB of anything is really radical.

I use all kinds of mics. I mentioned the AT5045s I'm using now, but I still frequently also rely on vintage U 67 tube mics, especially for strings. These days, I also like Royer mics a lot. I have a lot of Royers, both ribbons and tubes that I use frequently.

I love my Royer R-122 ribbon mics that I use on trombones, and on solo trumpets, like with Arturo Sandoval. It's also my favorite mic for tubas; to me, there's a warmth to it that enhances the sound of the instrument.

I also still rely on my tube AKG and Neumann microphones, but if I don't have the 67s around. I have Mojave MA-300 mics that I love as well for trumpets and saxophones.

I try new microphones all the time, but I'm also not afraid to use old mics. Some people don't like to do that because they're concerned, especially on big orchestra dates, that old tube mics may go bad during a session. But I don't worry about that. At Capitol, they take very good care of their mics. We rarely have a problem, and we also keep a spare sitting out ready and warming up. If we need to, we can change one out immediately without wasting any time.

I think about microphones a lot, and I still get excited by them. Like I said, they are both works of art unto themselves, and they're also the paintbrushes I use to help me get the sounds that I want.

LEAKAGE IS MY FRIEND: USING THE OMNIDIRECTIONAL PATTERN

I don't really have secrets but, if I did, this might be one. For about twenty years now, whenever I can, I prefer to use microphones in the omnidirectional pattern rather than the cardioid pattern. I find the sound in omni to be richer and more pleasing. These days, I use omni mics on vocals, strings, horns, violins, in big bands and orchestras—on almost everything, actu-ally—wherever possible. To do this requires a good-sounding room and good microphones, and it doesn't always work, but when it does, I prefer it.[2]

How did it happen that I started doing this? Well, I've told you how much I love microphones. I spend a lot of time thinking about how my sessions should sound, and at one point I decided that, in general, I just really like the way microphones sound in the omni pattern position.

It's common that we use microphones in the omni mode for room mics and overheads. Engineers have been doing that for years, with the mics set way up high in the air. For example, if you're using three Neumann M 50s in a classic Decca tree formation, they're all in omni. You wouldn't use a car-dioid mic in that context because you want to pick up the full sound of the entire room and a cardioid mic is directional, so it's rejecting the portion of the room sound that it behind it.[3]

I don't generally use a Decca tree; I just use two mics up high. But I started thinking about it. We're using the omni pattern on mics set up high to capture the sound of the room, and we add that into the mix. We like that sound; why wouldn't it work for closer mics, too?

When I started mulling this over I was working a lot at Capitol, where the rooms sound wonderful. I always aimed to capture as much of that room sound as possible, and it just kind of evolved from there. I knew that I liked the omni sound, and I decided to try it in different situations.

I started with trumpets on overdubs, and I liked it. Then, since trumpets are generally loud instruments and I wasn't too worried about leakage from the other instruments getting into the trumpet mics, I also tried it on the trumpet sections in full big band sessions. That sounded good, too.

It wasn't ever really a problem to experiment and try it out. Since we were generally using Neumann U 67 microphones on the trumpets, which have a built-in pattern selector, if it didn't work, we'd just have to go out to the microphone and flip the pattern switch back to cardioid. It wasn't like we'd have to tear down everything down and start over.

Next, I tried it on saxophones, and I thought that it gave me a better-sounding blend. Using, say, five mics in omni on the saxes, the leakage going into each mic on the sax section made for an overall richer, warmer sound

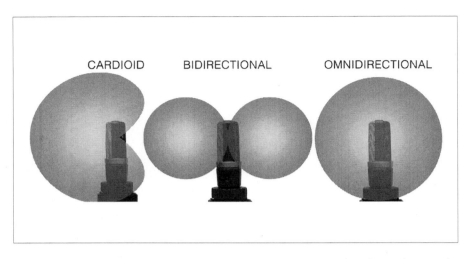

The three primary microphone pickup patterns: cardioid, bidirectional, and omnidirectional.
(Illustration by Bill Gibson)

with added depth. Then, since the results were good on trumpets and saxes, I started doing it on strings, for the overhead mics on the violins and violas, and then on the French horns and woodwinds as well. And I found that I consistently loved what the room sound added to the overall sound.

That's how it happened. By trying it out, a little bit here, a little bit there, I gradually eased into it. Since the results were so good, I kept using omni more often, and on more instruments. Then, I did a big band date where I put almost everything in omni, and it sounded amazing. These days, on big bands and orchestras, I start with it. It's easy. I don't really need to make any adjustments to my normal setup to use the mics in omni; the setups are pretty much the same ones I would have used anyway.

There are a few instruments that I don't generally use omni mics on. I use cardioid mics for cello and bass, because, if I have a brass section, the players are positioned so that they're blowing their horns toward the cellos and basses. Since we usually only have four basses and two cellos, or maybe only two and one, they don't have that much volume and I don't want all that brass leaking into them.

Also, in a big band, I don't use omni on trombones. For the trombones, I'll use bidirectional mics that are open on two sides, usually the Royer model 122 ribbon microphones.

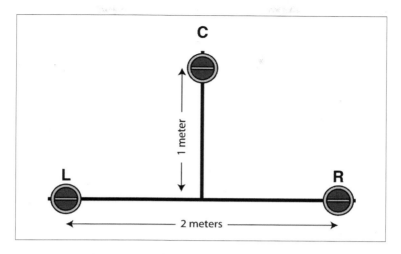

The Decca Tree.
(Illustration by Bill Gibson)

Occasionally, when recording an orchestra, I might find that I'm getting too much leakage from the French horns, and/or woodwinds, into the strings at a certain spot in the recording. If that happens, I'll ask the conductor to bring those instruments down a bit at that section, and he or she will do that for me. So, that gets taken care of out in the room. If you're working with a team, that's how it goes. If it seems necessary, we can always put the string mics in cardioid. And if we decide we want a little more isolation around an instrument, we can put gobos (fabric and wood constructions that absorb sound; also called baffles) around it. But that rarely happens.

Many people—and I was one of them—were taught from the beginning of their recording career that you didn't want instruments leaking into one another's mics. That's why iso booths were built in the studios, so that instruments could be kept isolated from one another.

I've thought about this a lot, and I believe that perhaps one of the reasons people started worrying so much about leakage, wanting a lot of separation on instruments, and using cardioid mics to get that separation, may have been because they were using cheap mics that didn't sound that great to begin with.

If the mic you're using doesn't sound good, the leakage you get in omni won't sound good, either. And bad leakage can be difficult, or impossible, to fix. Also, it's possible that if you're using a cardioid mic, the leakage into it may sound bad because cardioid mics are designed to reject the indirect, off-axis leakage. There are various ways cardioid mics are manufactured to reject that indirect sound, and some of the technology used to do that may make what leakage the mic does pick up sound bad. Steve Genewick, the engineer who has assisted me on so many sessions, explains it this way:

> One reason microphones sound better in the omnidirectional pattern is that all mics are inherently omni—except for ribbon mics, which are, by design, bidirectional because their ribbon is flat and only moves in a certain way: back and forth. If a mic is cardioid, or if it's a multipattern mic and you are using the cardioid pattern, something is being done to the design of the microphone that manipulates the sound to create the cardioid pattern. Whether it's the use of two diaphragms in the mic, with one turned off for cardioid, or it's a shift of the phase that cancels out the sound coming from the back, something is being done to create that cardioid polar pattern. So, inherently, frequency response is better in an omnidirectional mic because it is the natural state of the microphone. The cardioid pattern is designed to reject most higher frequency off-axis sounds. Individual mic designs vary in their ability to reject off-axis sounds, and all cardioid mics are omnidirectional in the lower frequencies. So, it stands to reason that the sound that does get through is affected by whatever that manipulation is.

A third reason you could get bad-sounding leakage would be because you were recording in a bad-sounding room. In that case, when the room sounds bad, you'll want to eliminate as much of the leakage as possible.

What's a bad-sounding room? Rooms that are so live that you have to struggle to keep some isolation, or rooms that are too dead, where you have to add echo to open them up. You don't want a note to come to the end of its sound and just quickly die; you want it to ring out into the room and sound complete. Also, some rooms may have too much low-end resonance and others may have not enough.

That's why the great acousticians, like the late Vincent van Haaff who designed so many good studios, are so important. They understand how to design a great room. It's vital, both in the studio and the control room, that you are able to trust that what you are hearing is accurate.

So actually, it's pretty simple. If you've got a good room, with good ambience and good mics, leakage is your friend. It adds to the sound rather than detracting, and using omnidirectional mics might be a good idea. Leakage can make your recordings sound bigger and more three-dimensional, because it helps everything blend together in a more natural way. You're actually getting the whole sound of the player, or players, in the room, not just part of it. But you've got to make leakage work for you and not against you. That's one reason I always use the best-sounding microphones possible. A poor microphone won't do the trick; the leakage will sound bad and then, you have a problem.

IN PHASE OR OUT: CHECKING POLARITY

One of the things that we do before the start of every session is to check polarity on the microphones to make sure they're all in phase. Years ago, the wiring was done differently at RCA's recording studios than at Columbia's studios—I don't know why. Each company just had its own way of doing things. But if you had a mic on your session at one studio that had come from the other studio and you didn't realize it, you had a problem. These days it's still really important, and mics and other equipment can be out of phase, with reversed polarity, more often than you would think.

Phase and Polarity

Phase refers to the timing relationship between audio signals. Electrically, if two identical audio waveforms are *in phase*, they follow the exact same path and, when combined together, double in amplitude (volume). On the other hand, if those same two waveforms are 180 degrees *out of phase*, they cancel completely because the positive energy (positive polarity) from the peak of the audio wave works against the negative energy (negative polarity) of the trough of the wave.

Acoustically, whenever two or more microphones pick up the same sound source from different locations in the room, there is a likelihood that the mics will capture the waveform at different points in its cycle. When this happens, the two waveforms shift in their timing relationship to each other and, when they combine together in the mix, the resulting sound can be

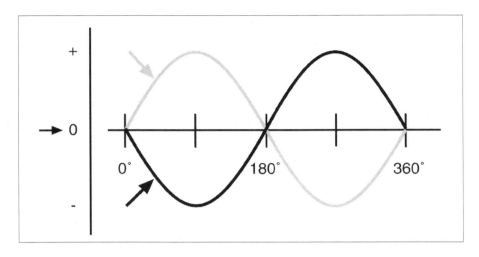

The gray wave and the black wave are 180 degrees out of phase—they are opposite in polarity.
Electronically, these two waves cancel each other, resulting in no sound.
(Illustration by Bill Gibson)

thinner and more hollow-sounding than it should be. When microphones, or their cables, are wired out of phase relative to each other, this problem is compounded. Phase shift, whether it's caused by an incorrectly wired electrical connection that reverses electrical polarity, or by a physical time delay due to the placement of microphones, can be very destructive to the overall sound of a mix.

If the sound waves captured by two different microphones are 180 degrees off from each other, which they can be if the electrical polarity of one of the mics is reversed, cancellation will occur. However, in reality, since the microphones are deployed in an acoustical space with its own unique blend of acoustic reflections, that cancellation won't be complete. The sounds captured by the mics might completely cancel at some frequencies and barely cancel at others—the actual results depend on the room, the distance between the mics, the characteristics of the mic, and the placement of the sound source in the room. In short, it's complicated!

If somebody in the tech shop wires a microphone or a cable incorrectly, and you don't find out before the session, it can really mess up a recording. If a mic's polarity is reversed, it will be out of phase with the other mics. They will null each other out at some frequencies, partially null at other frequencies, and you'll get a sound that is thin, unfocused, and just wrong. When you're working in a big room with a lot of mics set up and you have an out-of-phase microphone, you'll find that the overall level will be different than if everything is in phase with one another. Things just won't sound right.

Mic placement matters as well. You could have a phase problem between a kick drum mic and an overhead mic because the kick drum signal is arriving at the mic right in front of it instantly, but arriving at the overhead mic a little bit later. That can also make a difference in the overall sound. With experience, you learn to hear that kind of cancellation.

Sometimes, engineers will measure the distance between the drum overhead mics to ensure that they're equidistant from the snare drum so that the signal from the snare drum arrives at both at the same time. I don't do that. But we do use an electronic polarity checker during every setup, and, of course, we also listen.

The polarity checker has a clicker that we put in the studio, and a receiver that goes in the control room. When you open up the mic on the console, the receiver flashes red if the mic is bad and green if it is good. We do this on every session, even if there is only one microphone, because there could be something else besides the mic or mic cable that is flipping the polarity. There could be a piece of gear, or a cable that's broken or wired incorrectly. To ensure we don't have that problem, we check the entire chain from the mic to the recorder.

While we're doing that, we sometimes also find other problems. For example, if we have five saxophone mics that are all U 67s, and one of them is a lot quieter than the others, we know there's a problem. It could be that the pattern switch isn't set right. Or maybe there's a preamp or pan pot on the console that's got a problem and it's causing the level to drop.

For a session with forty to fifty mics, it usually only takes fifteen to twenty minutes to check everything and it's well worth the time. We do it at the end of setup when everything is already plugged in, and we listen through the chain: from the mic, into the console, into the compressor or EQ, if we're using any, and also into the tape machine or digital audio workstation (DAW).

Doing this is a regular part of every setup at Capitol, and we also do it when we work at other studios. You'd be surprised at how often we find problems.

EXTERNAL PREAMPS

I am generally working on consoles that have really good preamps and I use them a lot. But I also use external preamps quite a bit because I like their coloration and sound. I like the old Neve 1073 and 1081 preamps and I use them as much as I can. I also have a few of the Mastering Lab tube preamps that I love. I use them on trumpets all the time and they are fabulous. I have some Upstate Audio preamps that are terrific, but they aren't made anymore. The designer never really got a business going. The ones I have are a set of prototypes that he made and sent to both me and engineer Chuck Ainlay. He wanted them back, and I said, "No way, I'm keeping these!" I was ready to buy them, but in the end, he just left them with me. Only the prototypes exist. It's too bad, because they're really great and I use them all the time.

We're very lucky that in our industry, there are a lot of really knowledge-able technologists who are passionate about sound. Some of what they create is really high end and it costs a lot to design and manufacture. Some of their products make it to market and some don't, but all of us who are engineers appreciate their efforts.

DRUMS

For a long time, I used an AKG D112 on the kick drum. But then, I got a gift of an AKG D12, the original, older version of that mic and I liked it a lot. It's actually the fourth D12 ever made and now I mostly use that on the kick. I always mic the kick from the front unless there's some specific reason, such as they want to hear more of the sound of the beater itself actually hitting the drum. Then I might put a mic on the beater as well. If there's a hole in the drumhead, I'll put the mic right up by the hole. Not inside, just right up on it. And if there's no hole, then I try to center the mic and keep it a little bit away from the drum head.

On snare, I use a Shure SM57 under the snare drum and an AKG 452

AKG D12. (*Courtesy of Harman*)

with a 10-dB pad over the top. I'll put each mic on a separate track, and I'll put the 57 out of phase. You have to put the bottom mic out of phase, since two mics facing each other like that will most likely be out of phase and cancel each other out somewhat.

With the two mics, you get the actual sound of the snares from underneath the drum, and you can blend that in with the top mic. If you want more snap or crack from the top, you have it, but you can also add in as much of the sound of the actual snares as is appropriate for any particular song. In some cases, you may not use the bottom mic at all; for example, if the drummer is using brushes. But it's there if you want it.

AKG C452 on the top snare head and a Shure SM57 on the bottom.

On the hi-hat I also use an AKG 452 with a 10-dB pad. On the tom toms I used to use AKG 414s with 10-dB pads all the time; now I sometimes might use the little Audio-Technica 350 cardioid condenser mics with no pads.

You always want to make sure the drummer is all set, with everything where he or she wants it before you place the microphones. For toms, I get the mics close to the rim, at an angle facing toward where the drummer is going to be striking the drums. Again, you have to be careful to make sure you are not putting the mic where it might be hit. You don't want the drummer to be distracted because he or she is concentrating on not hitting the mic. It just stands to reason that when a drummer, or any musician, is distracted instead of completely focused on playing, you're not going to get his or her best performance.

AKG C414s on toms.

These days I use AT5045s on the overheads. When they came out a couple of years ago, I tried them, and now they're usually the only mics I use for that purpose. They're very clear and beautiful on cymbals. How high we place the overhead mics just depends on the sound of the drums and the overall kit itself. Sometimes, I still use my AKG C12 VRs, though.

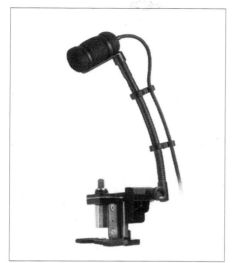

Audio-Technica ATM350.
(*Courtesy of Audio-Technica*)

AT5045.
(*Courtesy of Audio-Technica*)

I record from the drummer's perspective. I set the drums up on the console as if I was playing the drums myself and facing the control room, with the hi-hat on the left. It doesn't sound right to me to listen from the audience perspective.

Most of the time drummers show up a little early, and when they do, I always ask them to go out, bang on the drums, and just kind of whack them around a little bit so we can check each drum. If the drummer has a tech and the tech arrives first, we'll get the tech to play for a while. Or if my assistant can play, I may have him or her do it.

I'll listen to one drum at a time while they're playing. I'll make sure the levels are right so that each tom's level is evenly balanced with the others and that all of the individual drums sound good, with no rattles, or anything else going on that you don't want to hear. I check that all of the mics are working, that everything sounds in phase, and then I get a basic balance.

The kick drum is the first thing I listen to, then snare, then toms, then overheads. Then I listen to the whole kit and make adjustments until I get what I want. By the time we're ready to start getting sounds with the whole band, I've already got the drums pretty much dialed in. Of course, drum-

Setting the AKG C12 VRs as overheads.

mers play a lot differently once everyone in the band is playing, but at least I'll have the basic balance going.

I can get that basic balance with someone else on the drums, but, invariably, when the drummer comes in, he or she will move things and we'll have to go out and reset the mics anyway. Each drummer is a different instrument unto him or herself. No two drummers play the same; no two drummers sound the same; and no two drum kits sound the same.

While I'm getting drum sounds I'm hoping that everything is going to fit together with the band when I hear them start playing together. But inevitably, when the band and drummer do start to play together, it's a whole different thing—as it is for each song—and the drummer will be making his or her own adjustments. So, you'll often have to change things around a little bit as you go to have everything right for each particular song.

BASS

Years ago, I used just one mic on the upright bass, a tube Neumann U 47. But when I got a pair of Neumann M 149s, I started using both of them, in cardioid, one on the f-hole and one a little higher up on the other side near the fingerboard. It turned out bass players loved it. The great Chuck

Two Neumann M 149s on the acoustic bass.

Berghofer, for one, started thinking that I was the greatest thing since ice cream when he heard the way his bass sounded using both mics. Actually, in general, I think bass players are always happy to work with me, because it really is my favorite instrument. I love the standup bass and they know I'm going to get a good sound.

I do admit that standup bass is a difficult instrument to capture well, but I've got it down now. Like anything else, it takes putting the mics in the right spot and then listening to how the bassist plays. Are they going to do arco with a bow and then go to pizzicato, plucking with their fingers? In that case, you've got to place the mics back a little bit so that they don't get hit with the bow. Again, the best thing to do is ask the player what works for him or her.

When the bassist starts playing, I'll set my levels and make sure I'm hearing the full body of the instrument with the right balance between the lows and the top end. I place the mics in the right spot and I then put them into two Summit TLA 100 limiters and just tap them, so I'm barely moving the needle, for about a dB of reduction. That gives me some nice warmth from the tubes. If I have the Summits available, I will do that every time. If I don't have them, I'll use another kind of limiter to get that sound, but again, it's just for warmth. I don't really use any actual compression on bass mics. I take the signal just the way it is and just use the compressor to get the sound of its tubes.

You always have to pay attention to know where to put the mics to get the best sound, but also, you don't want to interfere with the musician. You don't ever want players to be worried about hitting mics and being the one who messes up a take because of that. You want them to be unaware of the microphones, and that's what we try to do. Often, you'll have a music stand to deal with as well, which is taking up space, so the player may not even have to see the mics, and they won't be a distraction. In that case, unless a bass player is looking down, he or she won't see the mic on the f-hole at all. That's a good thing.

RECORDING VOCALS

By now you know that I have quite a few favorite microphones that I can try for each singer. If it's an artist that I know, I'll already have a general idea of what will work well for him or her. But I also always have something else standing by so that I can make a quick switch if I need to.

These days, one of my go-to mics for vocals is Capitol's "Frank Sinatra" Neumann U 47. Well, as I mentioned, it's actually a 48, although we refer to it as a 47 because they look the same. The difference is, the 48's two patterns are cardioid and bidirectional, whereas the 47s are cardioid and omnidirectional.

I also often use the Brauner VM1. It's a very transparent-sounding, large diaphragm tube condenser mic with a continuously variable polar pattern; it goes from figure-8 to omni. It's built by Dirk Brauner, and it's inspired by the original Neumann U 47. It's definitely a very modern microphone but with characteristics of the U 47, U 67, and M 49. I found out about it when I was working with a big orchestra in Berlin on an album with songwriter Alan Bergman. Dirk knew I was going to be there, and he drove 250 miles to bring me a few to try. I did, and fell in love with them. Their noise floor is extremely low. In fact, once the setup was complete, I pulled up all of the room mic faders and could hear that the mics were active because they all put out a faint noise. But, when I pulled up the VM1 faders, there was such total silence that I thought the mics weren't working. I had an assistant go out and

Brauner VM1.
(*Courtesy of Brauner Microphones*)

The "Church" by David Pearlman.
(*Courtesy of Pearlman Microphones*)

tap on the VM1, and when he did, the diaphragms almost busted out of the speaker cabinets—they were on!

My third go-to mic lately is a tube condenser made by Dave Pearlman called the "Church." It's a remake of a microphone made for Metro-Gold-wyn-Mayer studios in the 1950s by Stanley Church, who was the studio's chief sound engineer at the time. It was designed as a custom U 47 for MGM and uses the same M7 capsule as the Neumann U 47.

I don't generally have mic preferences based on whether the singer is male or female. It just depends on the individual's characteristics. You don't want the artist to think that you're experimenting, but in some cases it's nice to be able to have a choice. At Capitol, I'll often set up all three of my favorites: the Sinatra mic, the Brauner, and the Church when I have a vocalist out in the studio getting ready to sing. We'll put the mics close together and check them out individually. I'll ask the vocalist to sing directly into each, one at time. Then, we'll pick the one we like the best and give it a try.

I'm also very fond of my own old U 47, and I now have a U 67 I'm in love with, too. How do I ultimately decide what to use? I guess it's instinctive by now. Sometimes, one mic might work just a little better on a vocal or an instrument than another mic. Often for me it's a spur of the moment decision: "Let's try this and see how it works."

What's most important is that the singer is comfortable. When you've been around as long as I have, the singers know what you've done and they have confidence in you. That helps. But conversely, knowing what I've done has a couple of times made a singer nervous! One artist I worked with was so nervous I seriously thought about walking out of the room and having the assistant record her vocal, so she wouldn't be intimidated. That's a tough thing to say, but it's true, and actually pretty funny, because for someone who sings as well as she does to be self-conscious was a surprise to me.

Singers are sensitive, and the best thing to do is to just make them your friends. It's not always easy for them to be out there alone in the studio with people watching them through the glass. So, you want to give them a sense of reassurance: "We're going to get this done, and I want you to be as comfortable as you can be. We're going to put the microphone here. It that's uncomfortable, we'll move it a little bit. We're going to make sure that you hear everything really well, and if there's anything you'd like to hear differently in the headphones, let us know." You want them to feel like it is their personal environment.

What they hear while they're singing is also super important. I work with certain assistants all the time who are really good with headphones. They have the job down, so that I don't have to be involved so much with that anymore. They're tweaking all the time that we're recording, actually mixing for the headphones and making sure that everything is right. It's good for the artist to have them do that, and good for the assistants, too. That's why I like to work with certain people at certain studios; I get to know them and what they are capable of. My assistants are good and they're always completely involved.

ONCE MORE, WITH FEELING!

Some singers have great voices and they sing the words they see on a piece of paper. Some singers have great voices and they interpret. Frank Sinatra, for example, always interpreted the story. He knew exactly why a song was written and what the meaning of it was. He also hung out with the writers and knew what had inspired them to write their songs. He had all that down, and it helped him to be the great singer he was. Barbra Streisand, Sam Cooke, and Diana Krall are other examples; they're really good at getting to the emotion of a song.

Sometimes the singers with great voices who just sing the words make great records that sell. But the really great singers are truly artists who know what the song means and why it was written.

SOME VOCAL RECORDING TIPS

Microphone Distance: About six to twelve inches from the singer is optimal. You can put your thumb on your nose and extend your hand (the universal sign telling someone to screw off!) and that distance is about right to start with. But, as always, it depends on the singer. I remember making a record a number of years ago with Levi Stubbs, the lead singer of the Four Tops. We had to back him two and a half feet off the mic, and he still almost knocked us out of the control room with the power of his voice. You just have to use your ears to ensure you're not overloading the microphone or the preamp. By experimenting and listening, you'll find a combination that gives you a good sound for each vocalist.

Playing and Singing at the Same Time: With Diana Krall, everything we record is live, and she's always playing piano and singing simultaneously. We may do a small fix here or there, but her records are all live performances. That's a situation where I can't keep the vocal mic in omni because of the piano. I have to put it in cardioid. I'll place it down a bit in front of her, since she has a tendency to look down while she's performing, and the mic is about six inches away from her. You have to pay attention, though, and observe any movements that the vocalist makes while playing, so that you can take that into account with your mic placement.

To reduce the leakage from Diana's piano, once it's miked I'll put blankets over it, or we'll use one of the specially made piano covers that also isolate the piano pretty well. I can still use the same mics that I like on the piano, but the covering helps me maintain separation between the vocal and the piano. That way, if we have to punch in a piano fix, we can do that and still keep the vocal we've recorded. If it's a vocal fix, however, we might have to punch both the vocal and the piano at the same time in order to keep the ambience the same throughout the recording.

If a singer is playing an acoustic guitar, the same rules apply. You have to work with the leakage and be careful, because you can't totally isolate the vocal from the guitar. Remember to use good microphones so the leakage is good. And be sure that the guitar is not overpowering the vocal so that you can maintain some control over each track.

Room Ambience: I've recorded vocals all over the world, and I can get a good vocal pretty much anywhere. But if at all possible, you want to be in a room where the ambience, the sound of the room itself, is pretty good. If the vocalist is someone who sings softly, it doesn't matter as much. That's because with a quieter vocalist, there will be less reflection of the voice coming back from the walls and ceiling of the room and the coloration of the room won't be as apparent. For singers with bigger voices, the sound of the room matters more. You want an open room with good ambience that can handle their sound level.

Here's something interesting I learned one day when I was working at Fulton Studio. I had a string date at nine in the morning, and it sounded great. We left everything set up, and the next day the same players came in. It was a continuation of the day before, and everything was set up exactly the same—the same mics, same seating, same players, same instruments. But it didn't sound the same. It didn't sound as good. That nice airy sound we'd had the day before was missing. I couldn't figure it out. The only difference was that it was raining on the second day. I finally realized that was it: the humidity and the atmosphere had an effect on the sound. Different day, different weather, different sound.

Headphones: Nine times out of ten, if you're working with a rhythm section and a vocalist, the vocalists will want to hear a lot of themselves, whereas the musicians will want very little vocal and mostly their own instrument in the headphone cue mix. I'll have my assistant work to make sure all the performers are hearing exactly what they need to in the headphones. What they hear is what they're playing to, or singing to, so the right mix is super important.

Working with the headphones also keeps the assistant involved in the session, and helps build rapport between him or her and the artists. That's a good thing. Years ago, I sometimes saw assistants sitting in the back of the room reading a magazine and it really bothered me. That never happens on my dates. I make it a point to totally involve my assistants in each project. That way, they not only learn, they also build relationships with the artists. Running the headphone mixes is a good way to do that. Of course, it also helps make the session go better because the assistant is paying attention to the mixes throughout. On my sessions, everybody is involved, and everybody gets respect for what he or she does. I think that's important.

Usually, we'll put some echo into the cue mix for the vocalist, and I'll often use two reverbs for that. For instance, if I'm at Capitol I'll use one of their fabulous live chambers along with an EMT 250 reverb unit. I just get a balance between them that I like.

ACOUSTIC GUITARS

With acoustic guitars, like any instrument, the most important thing is to find the sweet spot to place the mic. What is the sweet spot? It depends upon the instrument itself. It's the place that particular guitar sounds the best for that particular song. You have to listen and decide where you think it sounds the best, and that's where you put the microphone. Sometimes, it takes just moving it an inch one way or the other to find that spot. If you're having a problem, ask the guitar player.

Once you place the mic, go into the control room, open up the mic, and listen. Does it sound like it did outside? That's what you want. If it's not right, I'll go out and move the mic. And if it still isn't right, I'll change the microphone. But I always go outside and listen, then compare what I hear outside to what I hear in the control room. That's something I generally have to do myself. There aren't very many people I trust to do that for me.

For acoustic guitar, and electric guitar as well, there are two mics that I particularly like: The Audio-Technica 4080, which is a great ribbon micro-

Audio-Technica AT4080.
(Photograph by Bill Gibson)

Royer R-122
(Photograph by Bill Gibson)

phone that I also like on cello and trumpet, and the Royer R-122, also a ribbon. Both are fabulous mics and both companies are great. Sometimes I'll use one or the other, or I might use both: a Royer on the amp and the Audio-Technica on the actual guitar.

I do always try to put a mic on the guitar itself, even if it's an electric guitar, so I can get some of the strumming sound. You'll hear that on almost any big band record I've done that had an electric guitar—and there are dozens of those records. I'll put the mic on a separate track and I may use it or not.

Another reason to have that mic set up, even if it's an electric guitar, is that sometimes you have a guitar player who will be switching back and forth from electric to acoustic and you don't want to have to run out and change things every time. I'll put the guitar mic right in front of him for either electric or acoustic, about a foot from the hole, then listen and readjust if need be. Generally, we'll isolate the amp a bit with a gobo around it. We'll also put the amp a little way off from the player so that I can get a bit more separation from the rest of the instruments and keep the sound of the guitar amp from leaking into them.

If it's a jazz record, it's a whole different thing. I'll try to keep the guitar amp as close to the player as possible. When I'm cutting a jazz record, the musicians are generally all in the room together and sitting close to one another. What's coming though the amp is part of the guitarist's sound, so he or she will want to hear their amp sound. Also, on a jazz recording, the guitarist is probably not playing that loud, so I'm not as worried about getting too much of the amp sound bleeding into the other instruments' microphones.

I'll always move mics around until I'm happy with the sound, but if I'm working with a player like Dean Parks, for example, he'll put the mic exactly where he wants it himself. And I'm happy to let him do that. Dean knows where it should be, specifically, for each one of his guitars. A lot of the great guitar players are like that. They know the sweet spot to capture the sound that they want. And that's great. It makes my job a lot easier!

It's the same with a mandolin or a banjo, or just about any instrument. Move the mic until it sounds the same inside the control room as it does outside. Then, when we run the song down for the first time, I always record the rundown and then bring the musicians into the control room to listen. After they hear the recording, they often make their own adjustments. Or they'll tell me that there's something that they need or want me to change. By giving the musicians an opportunity to listen, you're working with them and you'll know that they're happy with how they sound.

If a musician has an instrument you've never seen, ask him or her the best place to put the mic. He or she will tell you what he or she thinks, and then you've got a place to start. Plus, by asking, you've made the musician your collaborator, and you've demonstrated that you respect his or her opinion. It's just common sense.

TRUMPETS

For solo trumpets, I know I'm generally going to use a Royer 122. It's a warm-sounding ribbon microphone that's become very popular with trumpet players. They all seem to want to use them and often they'll ask for them

One U 67 on each trumpet, set a little to the right.

specifically. Arturo Sandoval brings his own mic and it's a 122. So, that's a great choice for solo trumpet situations—which can get pretty loud.

If I have four trumpets in a section, I'll use Neumann U 67s, always in the omnidirectional pattern. I'm not worried about other instruments leaking into the trumpet mics; they're usually the loudest thing in the room anyway! Again, I prefer the way the mics sound in the omni position over the cardioid position because they have much more openness and depth. Trumpet players, if they're using a music stand, will lean a little to the right, so I keep that in mind when I'm placing the mics.

Trumpets, of course, also have mutes. There are all different kinds of mutes that change the volume level and give the instrument different coloration. There are bucket mutes that clip on, Harmon "Wow-Wow" mutes with two pieces so they can be used with the stem inserted in the bell or not, and there are some that add a kind of buzzy sound, almost like a kazoo. I don't change the mics for muted trumpets, but we try to know when the mutes are going to be used so we can adjust for level if necessary.

SAXOPHONES

I also love how the U 67 sounds on solo saxophones. I'll generally place it about the middle of the instrument and back a couple of feet away. A lot of

One Neumann U 67 on each saxophone.

the sound comes from that area in the instrument—from both the bell and the keys—so I put the mic where it can get the sound from both.

If it's a big band date and I've got five saxes, I will either use U 67s in omni, or, lately, I've been using the new Mojave MA-300 mics, which are really nice microphones. If I have five players, I'll put a mic on each one. Years ago, of course, I couldn't do that because we had a limited amount of inputs. But now I do, and that gives us a little more control for getting the correct balance.

The U 67s I use are the original ones from the sixties, tube mics with a power supply. There haven't been any new versions made yet. If somebody told me "You have to do this big session but you can only have one microphone," the U 67 is the one I'd pick. I think it is the most versatile mic out there. It sounds great on vocals, and you can use it on trumpets, saxophones, and upright bass. It's also good for violins; I use it all the time on violins in a section.

TROMBONES

In a big band, there are generally four trombones and they usually sit in front of the trumpets. Trombones have a slide and a bell; they are lower toned and not quite as loud as trumpets.

One Royer R-122 on each trombone.

I've been using the Royer 122 on trombones for a long time. It's a small mic and doesn't take up much room. Trombone players, if they have a music stand, will want the mic to their left. Often, they'll tell you what they think. While I'm putting the mics out they'll say, "Perfect" or "Move it up a little bit." They'll tell you exactly where it's best for them.

FRENCH HORNS

You remember my fear of French horns? Bob Doherty, who worked at Fulton Sound with Tommy Dowd, showed me exactly what to do. Since the bell faces backward, we'd put a hard-surfaced gobo behind the players. The players would actually be blowing into that gobo, with the mic in front of them facing the gobo so that it picked up the reflection off the hard surface of the gobo. The sound would bounce out from the hard surface and that's the sound that we'd capture.

I use Neumann M 149s on the French horns because they have a nice brightness to them. You can, of course, also mike the bell, and I have done that, depending on the situation. For jazz albums with a big band plus French horns, I'll sometimes mike just the bell so that I can have the same kind of presence on them that I have on the other instruments.

The bell gives the horn a very hard and present sound and the reflection gives a much richer, more open sound. You do have to be careful, though. Because, if there are mics on the bells of the French horns, the mics will be facing toward the front, which is the opposite direction from the other instruments that they're picking up, and therefore, they're" liable to be out of phase. If you pick the sound up off the reflection instead, the mics will be facing in the same direction and are not apt to be out of phase.

PIANO: THE MOST DIFFICULT INSTRUMENT

I think the piano is one of the hardest instruments to record. There are the transients—sudden changes in level and frequency—inherent to the instrument, but also, a piano's sound is very personalized to the player and to the brand of the piano. So much depends on the style of the player and whether it is a Bösendorfer, Steinway, Yamaha, or whatever, because the characteristics of each brand are so different. Of course, this is true with every instrument, but I think it is even more so with pianos.

I always want the piano open, using the big stick. I never use the piano closed, and I never use the short stick. At Capitol, we have a sleeve—a cover—that fits over the piano. It goes over the open lid and it has two holes, like portholes, on its side so you can insert the mics.

Before we had the sleeve, we used packing blankets over the piano, but the sleeve is a lot easier. It's really helpful in cases, like with a big band, where there is a lot of leakage from the other instruments coming in and you can't really control it. It also works to keep the vocal out of the piano mics or the piano out of the vocal mic, which is especially good if you are working with someone like Diana Krall, who plays and sings at the same time. The sleeve doesn't block the wood of the piano top, so you're able to get isolation, but you're also still getting the nice wood sound from the inside lid of the piano.

Whether the cover is on the piano or not, I generally put the mics in the same place. I use two M 149s in the cardioid position inside the piano, a foot and a half off the keys, spread apart over the hammers, one over the middle low end and one over the middle high end. Rarely, but sometimes, I'll put a third mic over the low strings—the bass end of the piano. That depends on the piece of music.

If we are recording a solo piano, I may use a different setup. Along with the M 149s inside the piano, I might use an AKG C24 or a Royer tube stereo mic—the SF24V—outside the piano to pick up more ambience. I'll put the mics on four tracks; two are the stereo from the M 149s, and the two other tracks are the stereo ambience tracks. That way, I have flexibility to use what I want from each for the blend.

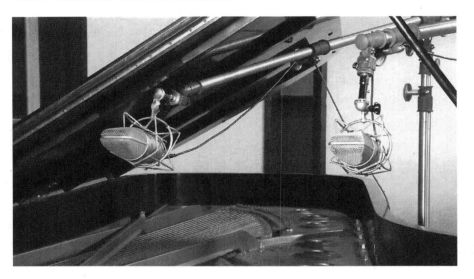

Neumann M 149s on the piano.

THE "AL SCHMITT STRING SOUND"

People do generally like the sound of strings I've recorded, but I don't think that there's really an "Al Schmitt string sound." As I've said before, I don't really have any secrets, and I'm always happy to share information about how I do things. I just love what I do and most of all, I listen. Here's my usual setup for strings.

If I'm recording an orchestra for sixteen or eighteen violins, I generally set up four U 67s in omnidirectional mode about ten feet up in the air. For the violas, the same. For the cellos, I use AT 4080 ribbon mics, one mic for each two instruments. There's usually one music stand for each two cellists to share, so I'll place the mic up above the music stand a little. I do that so it's out of the players' way, pointing down a little toward the cellos' f-holes, instead of it being crowded in by their knees, which would also be too close in to really sound good. You want a little bit of space for the mic to get the full resonance of the instruments. On the basses, I'll use Neumann FET 47s or tube U 47s. Usually, for four basses, I'll use two mics; one mic in between two players set back about three or four feet and aimed at the f-holes. Then, as always, you adjust.

Generally, once I've gotten all of the string mics up in the control room, and I've gotten the balance where I want it, the concertmaster will come in to make sure the blend sounds right.

I use reverb, just for monitoring, on the strings, and we listen to it that way in the control room. At Capitol, I use the live chambers. The string players aren't hearing the reverb in their headphones, though. Usually they'll just be listening to the rhythm section so as to keep time. But they'll tell us if there are other instruments they want to hear as well. They'll speak up and ask for more click or more drums, or whatever it is they need, and we give them as much as we can without hearing it bleed into the room mics.

ARRANGERS AND ARRANGEMENTS

I've worked with some of the great arrangers of all time: Henry Mancini, of course, but also Johnny Mandel, Pete Rugolo, Alex North, Billy May, Pat Williams, Claus Ogerman, Neal Hefti—who wrote the theme for the *Batman* TV series and the brilliant arrangement on Count Basie's song, "Little Darlin'," the one that is so slow. I recommend that you listen to the work of any of these arrangers; you'll learn a lot.

The writers, or composers, write the songs. They can sit at the piano or guitar, play the song and sing it. They are gifted with the ability to write great melodies and/or lyrics. Some of them are also arrangers. But in general, the arranger takes what the composer has done and figures how to do the song with the full instrumentation.

An arranger takes the song and sorts out the instrumentation: how many players, whether they'll use strings or brass, percussion, etc., and then writes out the notes and the charts. The arranger is truly one of the most important components of a recording. The arranger sets the tone and figures out what should happen in each section.

Then, the song goes from the writer playing piano and singing, to a beautiful orchestra with, say, Barbra Streisand singing. Arrangers are important, and they get paid a lot of money as well. While you could say that what they are doing is, absolutely, writing music, the difference is that they are not changing the original melody. Instead, they take the melody, and from that, they create the bed that the vocalist sings to.

The arrangement is also an inspiration to singer. When Claus Ogerman writes a great arrangement, for the singer it can be a "wow" moment. The singer has already run it down; he or she knows the song, and what he or she is going to sing. But then, when they're in the studio and they hear the arrangement, it lifts everything up. It puts a bed of beautiful music around what they're singing that sets a mood and helps to communicate the emotion of the song.

To do that, an arranger has to learn the range of every instrument, and how to write for them—trumpets, cellos, violas, harp, whatever it is. Usually the way it starts is that the arranger will sit down with the artist and the producer, or sometimes just the producer, to get some direction. For example, when I was producing Eddie Fisher, I would call Nelson Riddle or Hugo Montenegro and give him the key and a song demo so that he could get a sense of the song. Then, we'd talk over the meaning of the song and what we wanted to do with it. Of course, it depended on budgets as well, as to whether we'd use a small instrumental section or a big string orchestra.

There's that old saying, "Music hath charms to soothe a savage breast." And it's true. Music is one of the most important things in our life. The feelings it evokes affect everybody differently, but it affects everybody in some way. The arranger has a special role in bringing out that feeling.

What makes a great arrangement? What is it you're looking for? The fact that it is unique. There are a lot of big band recordings, but the ones that stick out often have outstanding arrangements. "Sing, Sing, Sing" with Benny Goodman is one of them. All of the work Nelson Riddle did with Sinatra, that's great arranging. It fit the song, fit the mood and fit the artist. If the song is an old standard, a great new arrangement will make it sound a little different than what's been done with it in the past.

I wouldn't exactly call it a lost art, because there are some really talented young arrangers coming up today. But, sadly, there's not as much of that kind of recording going on now as there was in the seventies and eighties. Back then, songs were often very dependent on great arrangements to fully realize their potential. If you listen to Johnny Mandel's "Here's to Life" with Shirley Horn, or the score Johnny did for the movie *The Sandpiper* with the song "The Shadow of Your Smile," and any of Diana Krall's recordings with Claus Ogerman, you'll get to understand what a great arrangement is.

BIG BANDS

Normally a big band is five saxophones, four trombones, four trumpets, and a rhythm section. But sometimes, there's more, like the album we did with Pat Williams called *Aurora*, where we had a big band plus French horns and percussion with timpani and chimes, all done live to 2-track. No going back and mixing! Peter Erskine was the drummer and it was a great band and a terrific album. You should check it out. (See Appendix B for a diagram of Pat Williams's *Aurora* sessions.)

As I've mentioned, when I learned to record, we had very few inputs on the console, so we didn't use a lot of mics. These days, I use more. Today, for trumpets and trombones with a big band, I use eight microphones, four for each section; back then I'd use two mics. The same with saxophones. Today, in a big band, I use five microphones on saxophones, one mic for each instrument. Back then, we'd use two mics for the five saxes.

Recording big bands is a lot of fun. Truthfully, the musicians do most of the work themselves. When a big band gets rolling along, there's nothing like it. When I'm in the control room, and we're doing the first rundown of the first song, I hear that sound coming back out of the speakers at me and I get goosebumps.

I love musicians, and when I'm doing a big band date, I walk in and give the musicians a big hug. They're always happy to see me, and I'm always happy to see them. It's just a fun thing to do.

Don't tell the people that pay us, but when I get in my car, and I'm going to do a big band date, or I'm working on a record with Diana Krall, as soon as I pull out of the driveway, I'm thinking, "Thank you, God, for letting me do what I do." Not too many people get to do work they really truly love. That's something I tell people when I teach: Don't let people discourage you. Follow your heart and do something you love. It makes life so much better.

MIXING: PHILOSOPHICALLY AND PRAGMATICALLY

I TRIED MIXING "in the box" with Pro Tools. It sounded good, but then I tried the same mix on an analog console and it sounded better to me. So, now I stick with an analog board.

We mix to Pro Tools at 192 kHz 24-bit; that's what we deliver to mastering. We started mixing at 192 a long time ago. Doug Sax, who was my mastering engineer for many, many years, got a converter for me that was made by Josh Florian, of JCF Audio, who at the time was also working for Doug. It sounded great and that's what we use still. We spent several years mixing to both analog and digital and comparing them. Digital kept getting better and better, and finally we just decided we liked the 192 mixes the best. Now, that's all we use. We record at 192 most of the time as well. For mixing, we come out of Pro Tools into the console, and out of the console it gets captured back to 192 on a Tascam DV-RA1000HD hard disk recorder using the JCF Audio converter.

Some engineers say that they mix by colors—they relate frequencies to colors and create their mixes like they're paintings. I recall working with Joni Mitchell, and having her ask for "more green," or "more blue." There may be a bit of that sensibility for me in how I'm feeling about the sound, but I don't see colors. What I'm going by is how I feel when I put all the parts in place. I keep working around with all the elements until I feel comfortable with what I have.

We joke about this all the time. Engineer Niko Bolas always says I mix with my heart. He's right. That's true in the sense that I mix with my emotions. I just keep trying things until a little bell goes off in my head that says,

"That's it." And that's where the mix will stay. It's just a matter of how it affects me emotionally.

I start from the bottom up, get the bass and kick where I want them, then add the overheads to where I like them. It's like building a house from the bottom up.

Tube-Tech SMC 2B multiband compressor.

When I mix these days, I have a three-band Tube-Tech SMC 2B compressor on the stereo output of my mixes, and sometimes I'll use it to compress the overall output a little. Again, pretty much, as always with me and compressors, I just tap it. With the three bands, I can compress a little on the low end, maybe less in the middle, and still less on the top. I just play with it until I like it. I also usually use an NTI (Night Technologies Incorporated) EQ3 that has something called an Air Band, to add just a little shimmer at the top. I'll also use the Sub Band on the NTI to give a little boost to the low end—one step of low frequency around forty or fifty cycles.

To decide when the mix is done, I usually go away from it for a little bit and then come back with fresh ears. Occasionally I may leave the mix up overnight. I did that on Natalie Cole's "Unforgettable." I was mixing at Schnee Studio in Los Angeles, working with David Reitzas as my assistant, and we were struggling to get a great mix. We couldn't seem to grasp it and I was starting to worry that they would take the mix away from me and give it to somebody else to do.

I went home, and when I came back in the morning, I asked Dave what he was hearing from the people involved. He told me the mix was still in my hands, so we went back to work, zeroed in, and an hour later we had the mix. We played it for everyone, and they loved it. We just needed a night away and for me to know that it was up to me to do it. That's another record you should listen to. It sounds really beautiful and I'm very proud of it.

Generally, though, I mix fast. I don't need to take a lot of time. If I'm mixing tracks that I've recorded, I can do three, four, sometimes five in a day. Because, when I'm recording, I'm already figuring out where I'm going to put things in the mix. I'm thinking way ahead, about the sound, the panning—and what the mix is going to sound like overall—the whole time that I'm recording.

It's a great feeling to be done with a mix, and to know it's good. I'm a happy guy then. I know we can send it to anybody and that we'll be cool. But I don't think there is such a thing as a perfect-sounding record. I've made records that won Grammys and made a lot of money, but I'll hear those records two years later on the radio and I'll always think I could have done them better. I don't think I've ever made a record I was 100 percent happy with. But I don't know if too many other people would say they have, either!

EQ

I don't use equalization (EQ) when I record. The reason I don't is that, when I learned, we only had one equalizer, a big thing that was made by Cinema Engineering for use in films. We were recording in mono then. The Cinema was in a rack and, if you patched it in because you wanted to equalize the bass, the voice—and everything else—got that equalization, too. That wasn't very helpful and we hardly ever used it.

Instead, we learned how to use microphones to get the sounds we wanted. Everything was done with mic placement. Just by moving the microphone, you can get a different sound from the drummer—or whatever instrument you're recording. If we wanted it brighter, we'd use a brighter microphone. If we wanted the sound to be a little warmer and rounder, we'd use a ribbon mic. So really, microphones are my EQ. That's how I learned and that's still what I do today.

These days, so many different varieties of EQ are available. But you have to remember that, in many cases, changing the EQ of one element changes its relationship to everything else that's in proximity to it. That's one reason I don't like it. I'd rather spend the time to put up a different mic, get a good, natural sound, and not have to use equalizers at all—not on the board or outboard, and not when I'm recording or mixing. The best signal path is often just the microphones, preamps, and faders; that way the sound stays cleaner. There are less electronics in the way, and you get more of the sound you're really looking for.

I think the bottom line is, sometimes records recorded without all of the extra electronics can sound bigger, and better. When you use EQ, you're potentially causing phase shift that can affect the sound. Sometimes EQ does things that, to me, aren't musical. I think some people don't realize how it can affect their blend overall.

For me, EQ usually just doesn't sound good to my ears, so I don't do it. I almost never record with EQ, and, if I'm the one who recorded what I'm mixing, I generally don't need to use EQ in the mix, either. It already sounds the way I want it to. The only time I'll use EQ is if I'm mixing something that somebody else did and I need to try to make it sound like what I'm looking for.

COMPRESSION

We also didn't have any compressors or limiters when I was starting out, so we did everything with hand limiting—for vocals and everything else. We just moved the faders and the knobs. Now, I do use some compression. I use it, but just a very little. On an upright bass, for example, as I've mentioned before, I'll have two mics; nice bright mics with a good top end. I'll put them in the Summit compressor/limiters and just tap them so the needle moves about a dB, and, since they are tube limiters, I get the warmth of the tubes. The same on vocals. I still ride the vocal fader with my hand, but I'll also tend to use a Fairchild 670, limiting maybe one or two dB, because I love the warm sound of the Fairchild and what it does to a vocal.

Back in the day, without compression or limiting, you had to learn the song as quickly as possible. Everybody was trying to get four songs done

The Fairchild 670.

in a three-hour session—straight to mono or 2-track, no remixing. What you heard was what you got, and you had to make sure you had control of the vocal. When the singers got big, you had to bring them back a bit, and then you'd push them up when they got soft so you kept them in range and avoided distortion. You didn't have time to make notes on when things were going to happen in the song. You'd just learn it all quickly during a rundown, and then you were in; you were recording the master.

Back then though, artists did tend to have better microphone technique. That's a bit of a lost art now; very few people have that kind of control anymore. I did several records with Rosemary Clooney. You could set the fader when she started singing, take your hand off, and just forget it—you could work on everything around her instead. She leaned in on the low notes, she backed off on the high notes, she knew how to lift her head a little bit when there was a *p* coming so she didn't pop the mic. Besides singing—and being a great singer—she did my job for me. She had fabulous technical chops, because she sang live all the time.

Sinatra was that way, too, and certainly Sam Cooke—I never used EQ or compression on Sam, not even in the mix.

PANNING

Panning is more important than you would think. I talk about this a lot when I'm teaching. One time, I was struggling with a mix. It was being very difficult, and I just couldn't get it right. Then I happened to move the electric guitar from one side to the other side and the whole mix opened up. It was like somebody opened a door. I was amazed at the difference it made to the overall sound of the mix to just move the placement of the guitar. Because, on one side it had been masking other sounds. When I moved it, it had more clarity and space of its own and wasn't clouding other things. The whole mix blossomed! That was a big lesson. Now, I advise people: if you are struggling, try moving things around—side to side or from the side to the middle. Don't just stay locked in.

What I used to do when I was mixing was to draw out a diagram: bass, drums, piano low, piano high, Fender Rhodes piano, electric guitar, and so on. I'd do this on a sheet of paper and keep it in the tape box to show how I'd panned everything on the mixes. That way, if it had to be recalled, we could see how I had laid it out and we could repeat it.

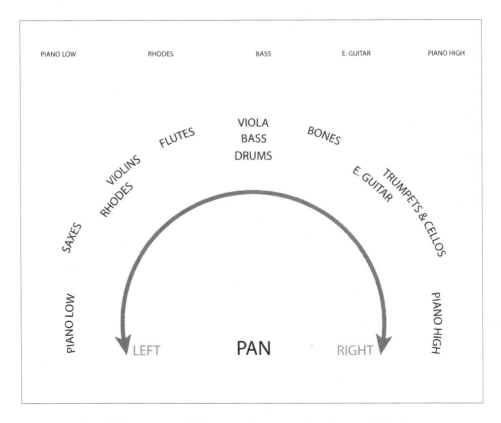

A sample of Al's panning notes for a typical session with orchestra and rhythm section.
(Illustration by Bill Gibson)

THE ART OF REVERB

When I was starting out and working with Tommy Dowd at Apex, we had a little room there that we'd shellac and use for an echo chamber. We'd go in there for twenty minutes and shellac away. We'd come out to get some air and clean our lungs out, and then we'd go back in and shellac some more until we'd put on eight or nine coats. We had a speaker and a mic in there, and that was our live echo chamber. That was the only echo we had. Electronic reverb and echo didn't exist yet. EMT plates didn't even exist. All we had was that live chamber that we made ourselves.

When I went to work at RCA in Los Angeles it had just built five live echo chambers. The rooms were all about the same size, and they all had the same speakers and mics so they sounded similar.

When we got to where we were working in stereo, I'd use all five chambers, one each for left, right, center, midleft, and midright. Whatever side my instruments were panned to, that's where their echo went as well, into one of those chambers. I'd put trumpets and trombones in one chamber, violins in another, vocals in the center, and so on. That way, the echo on the different instruments didn't bleed across one another; instead, it was discrete echo. If you listen to the Mancini records I did, you'll hear what I'm describing. I'd put the guitar, say, a little to the left, and then also put it into the chamber to the left so that all of the guitar reverb came back on the left. Panning things discretely like this into the separate chambers gave the instruments a lot of definition.

When I was a guest on *Pensado's Place*, we talked about this technique and Dave Pensado was surprised to learn about it. He tried it and told me later that he loved it and has been using it ever since.

Now that I have so many great digital echoes to work with, I don't really work that way as much anymore. But I still do use a bunch of different echoes and I still use live chambers. Now, with stereo chambers, I'll have, say, the guitar, panned a little to the left but the echo comes back on both sides. When I'm recording, I usually only use one live chamber, sometimes two, and they are used just for monitoring. But for mixing, I'll set up eight to ten reverbs in total.

Capitol has eight live chambers. They're all different sizes with different equipment in them so that they all have a bit of a different sound. I love them. My favorites are Four and Five, but I can't tell you why. They are all a little different, but it isn't really anything you can describe. I use Four all the time. Niko Bolas prefers Five, which is great, because if we're both working on the same day, we don't have to compete for a chamber!

I also love my Bricasti and use it a lot, along with the Lexicon 480, where I really like the Small and Medium Stage programs. I also like the TC Electronics M6000, and sometimes the "R2-D2 machine"—the EMT 250.

I still try not to put more than two instruments in any one chamber and usually I try to keep it to just one. That way, I can move the reverb parameters around and add more or less delay, or whatever I want, for individual instruments. If both the guitar and the piano are in the same chamber, what I'm doing will affect the sound of both, and I might not want that. That's why I like to keep everything as separate as I can. Violins in one, violas in another, panned left and right. The trumpets will be in one chamber, the trombones will be in a different one, and the saxes in a third. Doing this helps me keep clarity and definition. I'll change things if I want to narrow something down, but mostly, if the instrument is panned left and right, in the echo it comes back left and right. The vocal is in the center, but the chamber it's in comes back left and right.

It's convenient to be able to easily change the reverb length and delay on electronic reverbs, but, still, to me, nothing sounds like a good live chamber. There are definitely some great electronic chambers, but none of the simulations sound the same as the real room. But with a live chamber, the only way to make adjustments to the timing is to add delay, which we usually do with tape delay, meaning we send the signal to an analog tape machine to delay it before it reaches the live chamber. But that's it. Obviously, the electronic reverbs have a lot more flexibility.

On vocals, I always use two chambers. I'd say every vocal I've recorded in the last thirty years has most likely had a blend of two reverbs to get the sound I want. Generally, these days, the two will be a live chamber and my Bricasti. I have the natural sound of the chamber and usually the setting called "Warm Echo" on the Bricasti.

I set the live chamber first, then bring in the Bricasti or sometimes the

EMT 250. It's a matter of getting the right balance between whichever two I am using. That balance is never the same because each vocal and its timbre and decay time hits the reverbs differently. Also, the tempo of each song is different. I can't put a mark on the reverbs and say, "Okay, this is where my blend is." I have to listen carefully and slowly blend the two.

This is something I spend a lot of time on. I'll mess around with them until that little bell goes off in my head and I know that's where I want to leave it. I don't know what it is that makes that bell ring. But it's always a blend of the two. I just use my ears, and I think that's what everyone has to do. You can't just set something one day with a singer and think it will be right the next day with another singer. It's also not something you can really describe in numbers to someone. It's personal, and everybody hears a little differently.

Of course, all of what I've been describing here is for mixing. While I'm recording, I use just two chambers, and I use them only for monitoring; I don't record them.

MASTERING

When I started, there were no mastering engineers. Well, when I started, we were cutting direct to disc, so there was no mastering, either. But even after that, for a long time we, as engineers, did all of our own mastering and editing. There were no mastering houses that specialized in that part of the process.

Of course, over time, all that changed, and I was very blessed to work with mastering engineer Doug Sax for many years. His studio was called the Mastering Lab. I think the first time we did a session was in 1976, and I stayed working with him until he passed away in 2015. Sometimes, he'd just add a little air to my records, that little bit of top end way up around 20,000 cycles that gives recordings a kind of sheen or sparkle. Sometimes he'd cut my records flat. And, sometimes he'd tell me, "Al, you could do a better mix on this."

When he said that, I'd just have to say, "Okay, Doug." It hurt my feelings, but I would go back and do a better mix. Because he was right. He did that with lots of people. We knew that Doug loved us, and we felt the same way about him. When he told us we could do better, we knew he was saying it for our benefit, not for his own. He always wanted us to put out the best possible final product.

Occasionally, we'd get a reference disc back from Doug after he'd cut it, and he would have added something to it that we weren't sure made it better. I recall one occasion in particular, on a record we did with Diana Krall and Claus Ogerman. When Claus got his copy, he said to me, "Gee, Al, I like what I heard on your original mixes better than this."

It was only a little bit of EQ that Doug had added. So little, that it was even hard for me to hear it. But Claus did. I went to Doug and told him and he said right away, "Oh, I know what it is, no problem," and he went back, took the EQ off, and cut it flat.

Doug was an example of a truly great mastering engineer. He never tried to mold the record to make it sound like a "Doug Sax" engineered mastering. There are some mastering engineers who do that, but I try to stay away from them.

The other thing that I loved about Doug was, he was never trying to put as much level on the record as he could so that it would be as hot volume-wise as possible. That was not what was important to him. We've been having loudness wars in our industry for a long time, with everyone wanting to cut as hot as possible so they'll beat out the competition. Doug simply didn't care about that. He cared about the essence of the music, and that included its subtleties and dynamics.

7

PRACTICALITIES: A DAY IN THE LIFE

HERE'S AN EXAMPLE of a pretty typical work day for me. I actually wrote this quite a long time ago, but it's still a good example!

- At eleven a.m., I'm just leaving my house for the one-hour drive to the Sony Scoring Stage in Culver City, California. We have a three p.m. downbeat with a sixty-five-piece orchestra and we're recording three songs with a superstar singer who has the voice of an angel. She prefers to do her vocals live with the orchestra.

- My assistant today, Bill Smith, and I have been preparing for this session for several days, discussing what needs to be set up where and what mics to use. Bill had previously sent the physical setup and mic selection we'd decided on to the assistants at the studio, so when I arrive, the physical setup is already done—chairs, music stands, microphone stands, and mics. We also sent them instructions on how the console should be configured—as in, which inputs to use for the various instruments.

- When we get there, the first thing we do is fine-tune the microphone set up. Next, we check each mic out to make sure they are all working and sound right. Once they're in place and we know they're all working, we decide how they will be routed to the recorder. For example: tracks 1 and 2 are for bass, tracks 3 through 7 for drums, and so on.

- When that's completed, we set up the echoes we'll use for monitoring and playback, and decide what the headphone setup will be—meaning who will be hearing what instruments. Then we wait for the musicians to arrive and the session to start.
- The drummer shows up early, so we get a jump on the drum sounds. When the bass player arrives, we get him set up and ask him and the drummer to play a little for a sound check. We also do the same with the rest of the rhythm section.
- By the time the three p.m. downbeat arrives, everyone is in place and we start the first run-through. Since I've done so many of these kinds of sessions, I've got a good idea of where the mic preamp and fader levels on the board should be set and have already gotten that done, so off we go. I always record the first run-through. I can't tell you how many times that first run-through has ended up being the master take.
- Bill handles all the headphone mixes and he's good at it. He's mixing as we go along, and we almost never have a complaint. We then go through the process of multiple takes and, when we think we have enough, we move on to the next song.
- The musicians, and the rest of us, too, take a dinner break at six p.m., and we finish up with the orchestra at eleven p.m. After the orchestra is done, we do some solo overdubs with flute, harmonica—which we end up not using—and vocals. By one a.m., I'm in my car for my hour-long drive home. I'll start mixing these tracks at Capitol in Studio C in a few weeks, and the results will be in the marketplace in a few months.

THE TOP 11 THINGS ASSISTANT ENGINEERS NEED TO KNOW

The assistant engineer's role in a recording studio is a very important one, and being an assistant engineer is the best way to learn how to be a good engineer. A few years ago, I spent a lot of time questioning some of my colleagues to discover what their thoughts were on the most important things for an assistant engineer to know. These are all things that make for a better working environment. Here they are, not necessarily in the order of importance.

1. Assistants need to be well versed in the use of Avid Pro Tools. These days, it's also helpful if they know how to use other workstations, like Logic and Ableton.

2. Most of the good assistants are musicians in their own right. Being able to read music, and being a musician, really helps them. When we're punching in parts and have a score in front of us, knowing how to find the spots to punch makes a major difference in how fast we can get things done. Artists can sometimes be temperamental. They don't want to be wasting time while an assistant is looking for the top of the second verse, or for bar 84 or the third beat of bar 22. This needs to be done efficiently, and it's up to the assistant to get us quickly to where we need to be to be able to get the punches and fixes done.

3. This sounds funny, but it was brought up by almost everyone I talked to. Personal hygiene is very important. A good assistant smells good. Not necessarily with a lot of cologne, but he or she needs to have taken a shower, and to be clean. Nobody wants to spend ten or twelve hours in a small control room with someone who smells like an old goat. Take a shower, wear clean clothes, and keep the breath mints handy. And dress nicely. You can get by with jeans and a T-shirt; people don't expect you to dress up. But dress decently.

4. An important attribute for assistants is the ability to be transparent. When we need them, they are present. The rest of the time, they're in the background. So, really, it is: Stay in the background. If you see a problem, go up to the engineer at an opportune time and mention it. Then it's the engineer's job to take care of it. Just be aware of what is

going on around you. Try to keep your eyes and ears open, and to anticipate the needs of the artist and the engineer. And never display a bad or negative attitude; leave your ego at the studio door.

5. If you make a mistake, own up to it. Admit it right away. Come and tell me. You may have to take your lumps, but we will address the problem and then we'll move on. I will take the ultimate responsibility for the mistake. I'll explain what happened and we'll fix it. I don't want you to worry too much over it. It's over and done with and we move on. If you are worrying about the mistake you made, you're very liable to make another one right away. So, if you make a mistake, go and tell the engineer in charge. It will be straightened out, and then we get back to work. We're there to make a record, and we don't dwell on the mistakes that were made. It's like playing golf: You learn from your last shot, but you've got to focus on your current one.

6. Keep a good, legible, accurate track sheet and session notes. Nothing can cause more confusion or mistakes than a track sheet that is inaccurate or messy. You need to always make sure when you're writing things down or putting notes into the computer that you check in with the engineer and you know whether the track is DNU (do not use) or TBE (to be erased). Make sure that if you write something down as being on track 18, it really is on track 18. It will be a bad mistake if something gets erased by mistake because the track was labeled incorrectly.

7. Be able to make a good cup of coffee.

8. When asked a question by the producer or engineer, if you are not sure of the answer, say so. Don't volunteer information if you're not sure it's correct. You want people to be able to trust you, so be honest and don't guess. It is better to admit you don't know something than to give an incorrect answer.

9. Keep a notebook, and make diagrams of the session setups, the microphones used, how the board is laid out, the date, the name of the producer, the engineer, the artist, and the performers. That way, if we come back three months later for a follow-up to the session, it's easier to reset it all up. A notebook is invaluable. Someday you'll be thrown into a session on your own and you'll have that notebook to look back on and tell you what to do. The notebook is a big help to both the engineer you're working with, and to you.

10. Keep the food menu at hand and bone up on where you can get good pizza, chicken, sandwiches, sushi, salads and burgers, and so on. Being able to offer recommendations will be very helpful to the people you are working with. Food is very important on sessions and people will like that you know the good places to get it. And if you're the one running for food, make sure you get back on time with the correct order and the right change! This may seem like a little thing, but it is not. If you want to succeed, the people you are working with need to know that they can trust you to get the details right.

11. Keep the studio neat. I, personally, hate to see things lying around. Having a neat working environment makes everyone feel better. And wrap up cables the correct way! It really bothers me to see people wrapping cables the wrong way. When I was eight or nine, my uncle would always get on me if I did it incorrectly. He'd say, "Is that the way I taught you to do it?" "No." "How did I teach you to do it?" "I forgot." "Okay, I'm going to show you one more time." Taking care of equipment properly was very important to him. And now, it is to me, too. So, wrap those cables so they are not kinked. It's over/under, then take the end and loop it through so that when you put it down, it doesn't come unraveled.

TAKING CARE OF BUSINESS: MAKING DEALS AND GETTING PAID

For producers, the first thing I'd advise is to get a good attorney to make your deals. It is definitely worth the money it costs you; don't try to do it yourself. Al Schlesinger, one of the best, was my attorney for many years, and he did all my production deals.

I know that these days, with the way the industry has changed, some people have given up on the idea of royalties and don't bother to negotiate for points—the back-end percentage that producers traditionally received. But I don't think they should give up. Even as an engineer, on certain projects you may be able to get points. It's true that much of the time it doesn't turn out to be a lot of money—if anything. But it's still something, and you never know—sometimes a record explodes, and it will become a big hit.

With budgets as small as they often are these days, it's understandable that people don't want to pay an attorney to draw up a contract, or for a representative to negotiate for them. But you can get an outline drawn up, or a model contract that could be used for most projects with the specific details adjusted. You could get it updated every few years, and then you would only need to use the attorney when you have something complicated.

But it really is best to have a manager or a representative doing the deals for you. You never want to negotiate directly with the artists, and the artists are never the ones who really negotiate anyway. It will generally be their management, whose job is always to do the best they can for their artists, and who therefore want to give you as little as they can.

Also, your representative will chase the money for you, which is sometimes something you really need. Doing that can be very time consuming, with letters and phone calls back and forth. If someone is working for you and getting paid when you do, he or she wants to make sure you get the money and will stay on it.

For engineering projects where I'm just getting my normal rate, I don't need someone to make a deal for me and I will do it myself. I just tell them the amount, and that amount can depend on the project and their budget. There are certain artists, especially in jazz, that I want to work with, but their budgets are small. So we just work something out together.

One thing people starting out often don't understand is that you can't sign on with managers or get representatives and just expect them to get you work. They can help get you get work, but that's after you've established a good reputation and accumulated credits. Until then, they've really got nothing to work with.

Work comes from projects you've done and people knowing about you. It also comes from getting to know people. I got work more than once from people seeing my road cases with my name on them in the hall at Capitol. People would see my name and they'd think, *Al Schmitt, he'd be great for that.* And they'd come into the studio where I was working and ask, "Hey, are you busy next Tuesday?"

Working at a multiple-room studio is good for that, although I know that these days, many people don't get to do that very often, and that's a shame. It's also great to work at a big studio because you get to see your fellow engineers, chat with them, and keep up on what's happening with everyone. Another good thing is seeing all the musicians and keeping in touch with them, because musicians will recommend you. When they know they're going to be working on a record, they may say to the artist, "Elliot Scheiner would be a great engineer for that." And then Elliot gets a call. Being out and about and networking is really important. Plus, it's fun. I enjoy it.

AUDIO MANUFACTURERS ARE YOUR FRIENDS

I love microphones, and I also love the people who make them. I like getting to know them. I mentioned that Dirk Brauner drove 250 miles to bring me mics to use in Berlin; and Neumann, Audio-Technica, and the other manufacturers, too, are always helpful if I need anything.

Relationships like that are important. When you get to know people, they will help you out when you need something. If I'm in a studio that doesn't have Royer ribbon mics and I want to use them on a couple of things, I get in touch with John Jennings at Royer, and he gets me some quickly.

It's the same with speaker manufacturers. If I'm working somewhere, and it turns out they don't have speakers I like, I can call Peter Chaikin at JBL and he will get me something that I'll be comfortable with to do my sessions.

These relationships also help keep me in touch with what's new. There are so many great mics, and other kinds of gear like preamps and compressors, coming out all the time. When you're close with the people who make the gear, they'll keep in touch with you about their products and you'll get the opportunity to try new things.

It's not just business; you become friends. I was teaching at a seminar, and John Jennings volunteered to come by and lead a two-hour class on how ribbon mics are made, and how they function. He had even me riveted, it was so interesting. Wolfgang Fraissinet, the head of Neumann, has been a dear friend of mine for thirty-five years. I'm truly interested in what they do and vice versa.

Relationships are a big part of our business. Working with the manufacturers this way is symbiotic; they help you when you need it, and besides the fact that you, yourself, are using their products, you are helping them out. Because when people see you using certain mics, they may also try those mics and buy them.

I've had situations where on certain voices nothing was working like I wanted it to, and Dave Pearlman loaned me his Church mic. I put it up, and it was, "Wow. That's it." I use four M 149s on sessions all the time; two on upright bass and two on piano, and wherever I go in the world, Dawn Burr from Neumann will get them there for me. That's because I have a relationship with them that benefits them as well as me.

In the audio world, there is a community of people who get very excited about the work that they do. Like I said, I love the mics, but I also love the people who make them.

8

ARTISTS, FRIENDS, AND MENTORS: WHAT I'VE LEARNED

SAM COOKE

I was Sam's engineer at RCA, and I learned a lot from seeing how he followed his instincts. He'd come in with a song he'd written, and he knew how he wanted the arrangement laid out. He'd talk to the arranger himself to get all that done the way he wanted it.

Another thing about Sam, he was happy all the time. For him, it was all about the music and how it would make you feel. I don't think I ever had a session with him where he didn't have a smile on his face and really, just a great happiness and warmth around him. He was also always well dressed. He always looked nice.

Everything certainly wasn't perfect for Sam. He'd had great tragedy in his life: his two-year-old son had drowned in the family swimming pool. But, in general, he didn't let things bother him. He was basically a very happy, positive guy.

He was also a great writer. Almost all of his hits were songs that he wrote himself, except on the live album I produced for him, *Live at the Copa*, where he did "Tennessee Waltz" and some other cover songs. He had so many hits: "Another Saturday Night," "Cupid," "Bring It On Home to Me," "Twistin' the Night Away," I worked on all of those songs with him as his engineer.

Then I got promoted up to producer, and when Sam's producers—two guys who were a production team called Hugo & Luigi—left RCA to start their own label, Sam told my boss he'd like to work with me as a producer. The truth is, producing Sam Cooke was a walk in the park. He wrote great songs, he had a great voice, and the music was always cool.

You didn't have to look for songs for him because he wrote his own. You didn't have to find arrangers; he had a group of arrangers he'd worked with forever and he always used them. And he sang well. We'd do two or three songs in three hours, with everything completed. It would be a rhythm section—two or three guitars, bass, drums, piano—sometimes a couple of horns, and sometimes, not too often, strings.

When we did "Bring It On Home to Me," he had Lou Rawls sing the duet parts with him, both of them live on U 47 microphones. They sang into the two mics right next to each other, facing the band. It was a ball to work on. Everything was live out in the room with the musicians, and we were chatting back and forth with them. I'm pretty sure that session was bass, drums, two guitars, and piano. Sam and Lou were in the middle of the room, and we set up a gobo behind them to keep some of the reflection from the instruments from coming into his mic.

Working with Sam was another of the great joys of my life. I was with him the night he died. We had dinner at Martoni's, which was the big hangout in those days, and we were talking about what we'd do for the next record. He wanted it to be a blues album, because he'd done a version of the blues song "Little Red Rooster" that was a moderate hit for him. Over dinner, we made plans that I'd come to his house on the weekend and we'd start going over material.

I had another artist, named Stan Worth, who was playing that night somewhere else, and after dinner I had to go over to see him. I told Sam I'd meet him later at P.J.'s, another watering hole for music people where Trini Lopez played. I went to see Stan, talked to him for a while, and then I went over to P.J.'s. I stayed until about twenty after one, but Sam never showed up. Later, I heard he came into P.J.'s with a girl around a quarter to two but the bar was ready to close so they didn't let him in.

The story we heard was, he took off and went to a motel with the girl. I was at home, sound asleep, when the phone rang. It was my good friend Lester Sill, head of Screen Gems, and he said, "Al, I hate to wake you, but I have to tell you Sam Cooke has just been shot." I said, "Oh, no, where is he? What hospital?" and Lester said, "No hospital, he's dead."

A few minutes after that, the phone started ringing. I got calls from New

York, London. Everybody was asking, "What happened?" Sam was a big, big act and everybody knew him.

He'd been shot by the manager of the hotel, and it was never really clear what had happened. There is still a lot of mystery and controversy about that night.

Sam started out as a gospel singer, and I guess you'd call what he did R&B, because he was black, but I never put a name on what he did. He could do anything. He was one of the greatest singers I've ever worked with. At the time, Sam and Frank Sinatra were the most imitated singers in the world. Sam's pitch, his phrasing, his tone, and his sound were stellar. There was the most gorgeous quality that came out of his voice. You really have to listen to his records.

He was also always a real professional. He came in prepared to work. His business partner was J. W. Alexander, a wonderful human being, who also always dressed nice. J. W. was a very bright guy and they had published all of Sam's songs themselves with Kags Music. Sam had everything. He was successful, famous, wealthy, and a chick magnet, too. Girls loved him.

We spent a lot of time together in New York when we were getting ready to do the *Live at the Copa* album. Sam had a suite at the Warwick Hotel, and one afternoon I went over and hung out there with him and Cassius Clay. He was still Cassius Clay then; it was a little while before he won the Sonny Liston fight, announced he'd joined the Nation of Islam and changed his name to Muhammad Ali. He was signed to CBS Columbia and was making a comedy record called *I Am the Greatest*. But there was one song on it, a version of "Stand by Me," and Sam was helping him with the vocal phrasing for it. There was so much fun, laughter and teasing going back and forth between those two; it was really funny. It was one of the best afternoons of my life.

Sam and I had just done the *Live at the Copa* album before he died, and that was kind of a change for him. The label was trying to get him into more of a smooth Nat King Cole kind of style, but of course, it never happened. Neither did the blues record we were planning.

What did I learn from Sam? I was in my early thirties when I was working with him. He had so much confidence in everything he did; maybe some of that rubbed off on me. My uncle and Tommy Dowd both also had a lot of confidence. I was lucky I had them all as role models. I see in a lot of assistants that they are hesitant and always asking questions. Questions are fine, but it seems sometimes as though they don't have the confidence to just go in and nail the job.

Of course, it takes time to get that ability. Being around recording from seven years old, I learned a lot from the engineers I worked with. They knew what they were doing and they also knew how good they were. They were confident in their own skills. I think it is a combination that builds on itself: experience gives you the confidence in yourself that you'll be able to succeed with what you want to do. Sam had all of that and losing him was a real blow.

HENRY "HANK" MANCINI

There was so much class and style in the way Hank Mancini worked. Here's an example. Hank preferred to work at night, from eight to 11 p.m., and Dick Pierce was his producer. By two or three minutes to eleven, we'd always have the take we needed; we were done for the night. Hank conducted, so he would be out in the studio with the musicians, and from the control room, we'd hit the talkback mic and say, "Great, Hank. Thanks, man. That was perfect." Inevitably, he'd reply saying something like, "No, not quite perfect. I heard something in the violas over here; we've got to do one more take."

Well, in those days, if you went one minute late, you'd have to pay everyone a half hour of overtime. And Hank would go over a little bit, all the time. It was his way of saying, "Thank you," to the players. Almost every single session, we'd be done right before eleven p.m., but then he'd be out in the studio saying, "I want to make a little change here," and then we'd go those few minutes into overtime. Everybody knew what he was doing, and the musicians loved him for it. Of course, it drove Dick Pierce crazy, because, as the producer, it was his job to keep the budget down. But after a while, it pretty much became the norm and we just assumed it was going to happen.

Hank was one of the most versatile arrangers of all time. He could do any style. His arrangements were also unique, and he went all out for the music. When we were recording the soundtrack for the film *Experiment in Terror*, for example, Hank had a giant organ brought in. It was a big deal to get it into the studio, and all the organist did, from the first part of the song through to the end, was put his foot down on one of the pedals and sustain a particular note. That's it. All that work and cost to get the organ there, for one note. But, actually, it was brilliant. Because, that low note the organist played was the threat and tension that flowed throughout the entire piece.

Hank loved to use unusual instruments—like that organ, and those thumb pianos and bass flutes on *Hatari!*—in unusual ways. He was a genius at incorporating them into his arrangements, and other people in the business appreciated what he did. All of the top guys worked with him—Shelly Manne, the great jazz drummer who could play in so many styles; saxophonists Gene Cipriano and Ronnie Lang; so many others. All the best musicians in the business loved him. And I felt the same way. Working with him was definitely one of the highlights of my life

Working with Hank, also, I have to admit, made me a little bit cocky. Somehow, even though we did such outrageously different things all the time, going into the sessions, there was never any fear. I went into every date with anticipation and the feeling that I was going to kill it. I'd be thinking in advance about how I'd set things up and what mics I was going to use and I was never worried about how it would turn out. I just knew that I was going to get it right.

If I had to choose, I think I'd say the biggest lesson with Hank was the way he handled people, and how much everybody loved him. All of the stars from the movies he orchestrated would come to the sessions and sit with us just to hang out. It made them feel good just to be there. And that's also how the musicians and all the rest of us felt as well.

JEFFERSON AIRPLANE

The group dynamic of Jefferson Airplane was wonderful. Marty Balin and Grace Slick sang so well together; they really had a sound. Paul Kantner was the main leader of the band—if you could say their brand of chaos had a leader. Paul wrote, sang, and played rhythm guitar. Jack Casady was on bass, Jorma Kaukonen was lead guitar, and Spencer Dryden was on drums and percussion. Grace played piano, recorder, organ and sang.

They all got along. There wasn't a lot of bickering. The band members all seemed to respect one another, and I liked that. But there's no question that their work ethic was insane—as in, I was constantly herding cats to get the records made.

I first saw them perform before Grace had joined the band. Signe Anderson was their first female singer and she was with them the first time I saw them. There was a huge buzz about the band, and RCA sent me up from Los Angeles to San Francisco to see them. When I got to the venue, which was a small club, there was a line around the block waiting to get in. I saw the show and I gave RCA great reviews on it. I liked everything about them. They were different, their songs were good, and they were very much what was going on in San Francisco at the time. I didn't know if RCA would want them, but I thought they were terrific and recommended them.

The next thing I knew, RCA had signed the band and they were making their first album, *Jefferson Airplane Takes Off*, with Signe singing. But that record didn't succeed in capturing them very well.

Grace joined for the next album, *Surrealistic Pillow*, which was produced by Rick Jarrard. Rick was a really good producer whose office was next to mine at RCA. He'd signed Harry Nilsson and produced all his early records on RCA. He also produced "Light My Fire" with José Feliciano, which was a hugely popular record.

Surrealistic Pillow had two giant hits, "White Rabbit" and "Somebody to Love." It was a big record for the band, but they hated it. They weren't happy with the way it sounded. They complained a lot about the echo Rick had used and they decided they wouldn't do another record with him. Since they were signed to RCA, and therefore had to use a staff producer, they said, "Well, we've met Al Schmitt and we like him. What about Al?"

So, there I was, producing Jefferson Airplane. The first day I worked with them was the first day of recording for *After Bathing at Baxter's*. I remember walking in and they had everything already set up, including a nitrous oxide tank and a little basketball court at one end of the studio. This was not normal for those days. It was totally crazy. We got started, we worked for a few days, and we really weren't getting anything accomplished. But they were comfortable with that, and I decided I would go along with them. I wouldn't try to push them too hard to work within a standard sort of process. Instead, I'd just have to try to find other ways to make them be productive.

At first, instead of telling them what they had to do, I tried to be diplomatic. I'd say, "This take is pretty good. We could probably fix it." But then, of course they'd respond, "No, we don't have to fix it. It's fine." So, that didn't work. But I still felt that it was important that I didn't put a lot of pressure on them at that point. I was trying to ease them into it and to figure out what we would have to do to get the record made. In the meantime, it just got crazier. I'd be at the studio at RCA in Hollywood at eight o'clock at night and I'd get a call from one of them asking, "Hey Al, are we working tonight?" And I'd say, "Yeah, that's why I'm here. I'm waiting for you guys."

"Ok, we'll get the next plane down." They were calling from San Francisco! They'd totally forgotten, until some one of them, I guess, mentioned, "You know, I think we're supposed to be working with Al tonight." A couple of hours later, they'd show up at the RCA studios and we'd work until five in the morning. And little by little, we were getting the songs recorded.

Another thing that happened on that album, you may remember, was that, in the first third of it, I quit RCA. But, pretty quickly, the Airplane had ended up hiring me back as an independent producer.

At the time, my brother Richy was also an engineer on staff with RCA, and he actually did most of the engineering on *Baxter's*. He also did most of the Airplane's live recordings in San Francisco, and when we went to New York to record, he came with us as well. Richy was a really good engineer and very easy to get along with. Being from New York, he and I were stickball fans, so we taught everybody in the band how it was done and we'd play games with them in the RCA garage after everyone else in the building had gone home.

Pat Ieraci, who was credited on the album as, "Maurice at the 8-track," ran the tape machine, and he'd play stickball with us, too. Pat's main role at first was tape op, but he was also into archiving and cataloging the tapes, and ultimately, he became really important for keeping things together. He never got high, ever. Eventually, he quit RCA and went to work for the band, and it became the three of us together—me, Richy and Maurice—trying to keep things going. The band loved Richy and they liked the fact that the three of us got along well as team. We were their anchor.

Truthfully, it was a lot of fun, but it was also really difficult, because it was my job to move the project forward. They'd start to work, if I was lucky, at eight p.m., and be there until four or five a.m., but often, we wouldn't get anything real accomplished. I remember marking tape boxes "Take 132" while we were trying to get a rhythm track on one song done—132 takes of one song. A lot of the music was written in the studio, and we never erased anything.

It was frustrating, but a lot of what they were doing was experimenting. They wanted a different kind of album than the two they'd made before. It was also just an enormously creative time in general. The world was changing dramatically, and the musicians and music of the time had a big influence on the culture.

The Airplane was hot, and everybody wanted to come to their recording sessions. Their fans were made up of all kinds of artistic people. Filmmaker Jean-Luc Godard would come by to hang out. On Thanksgiving, he gave us a private screening of his newest film, *The Last Weekend*. It's a famous, classic movie now, where the last automobile that can fit gets on the road, there's total roadblock, and nobody can move—it's the end of the world. We had Rip Torn and his wife visiting, we had Mama Cass there, and Janis Joplin—recording with the Airplane was a social event. We'd get a little work done between eight and eleven p.m., and the next thing you know somebody would drift in—maybe David Crosby with Joni Mitchell, when she was just starting out, then somebody else, say, Woody Allen, would drift in, too. We'd be working—or trying to—but when their guests arrived, all productivity would just die. Because everybody was getting high. I was the one always saying, "Hello folks, I'm trying to get a record done here!"

Grace was really the best of them, though. She was so bright and beautiful, and when there was a lull, I could count on getting her into the studio to actually do some work. She was always willing to do whatever was needed. She was in there with the craziness, but she also realized that they needed to make the record. I'm not sure the rest of them really thought that way. Grace was just more practical. And she was smart, a Vassar girl, you know. But she couldn't control them, and she didn't really try. At any given moment, you never knew what would happen around them. It was 1967, the year of the

Summer of Love, and they were of their times. It didn't matter to them at all that the studio time was costing money. They'd just be there. Talking, getting high, and hanging with all sorts of people.

Ultimately, somehow, we did get *Baxter's* done. It took five and a half months to make a record that should have taken two or three weeks. They just didn't care. They'd had two big hits, they were popular, and their whole attitude was based on being against what was the political status quo at the time—what they called "the Establishment." The title of Paul Kantner's later solo album, *Blows Against the Empire*, pretty much summed up what their point of view was at the time.

Baxter's came out, it did well, and we kept working together. In 1969, we did *Volunteers* at Wally Heider Recording Studio in San Francisco. It was actually the first album ever done at that studio. We were working in one room and the second room wasn't finished yet. Jack, in particular, was legendary for playing loud; during *Volunteers* we finally had to put his amps in that unfinished room to get them away from us and give the bass some isolation.

The Airplane's volume overall when we were recording was always pretty overwhelming. It was the same volume that they played at onstage. But we were trying to capture this in the studio, and on *Volunteers*, the bass was coming into everything. Back then, there weren't vocal booths or drum booths; everything was one room. You had some gobos you could use, or some blankets, to try to dampen down the sound, but that was it. Gobos and blankets simply weren't sufficient for Jack Casady's amp sound. Luckily, at Heider's, we were able to put him in another room and that helped a lot.

Volunteers was another wild recording. They were still totally crazy, but they were also absolutely serious about being counterculture and antiestablishment. Those were revolutionary times, in a sense, and they weren't kidding with those records. They believed in what they were saying. And they did help change the world, or at least the United States, and probably some of the rest of the world, too, at that time. That's what their *Volunteers* album was all about.

A long time after we'd made the records, Grace said to me, "I want to thank you for saving our asses." And it's true. I did. I was like the dogcatcher with a butterfly net trying to capture people and get them to work and actually accomplish stuff. But there were so many distractions every day. Grace would come in dressed in her little Girl Scout outfit—that was a sight to see. One night she came in dressed as a nun, and Spencer Dryden, the drummer, came decked out as a cardinal. They took a photo with her bent over the piano and him standing behind her and they wanted to use that picture for the album cover. I'm not kidding. This is what was going on.

I was independent when we did *Volunteers*; no longer an employee of RCA, and when I finished mixing the album I sent the tapes back to the label in New York. But when the RCA executives listened to it and heard the words "Up against the wall, motherfucker" in the song "We Can Be Together," they called me right away and said, "No. You cannot do this. No way. They have to take this off the album. They have to change the words or we're not putting the album out."[1]

The label was insisting, "No way." So, I gathered the band together for a meeting and told them what happened: I'd sent the master tapes to RCA, they heard what's been going on with the lyrics, and they refused to put the album out the way it was.

The band's response to that was, en masse, "Fuck 'em. Don't put the album out." So, I called New York and said, "Okay, don't put the album out. They don't care and they are not going to change it."

Six months later, the album came out in its original form—exactly the way the band wanted it. That taught me a big lesson. The truth was, the executives at the record company really didn't care about the language. They were shocked when they first heard it, but as a practical matter, all they really cared about was sales. What it came down to was, Jefferson Airplane was selling a lot of albums—a million or more—and all the label wanted to do was to get the record out and collect its money. So, that's what happened. The band got their way and the album we sent to RCA was the album that was released.

The Airplane's live performances were powerful, incredible really. They'd be tuning up on stage forever, and all of a sudden, wham. I used to love to go to their shows. We recorded one album, *Bless Its Pointed Little Head*, live at both the Fillmore East and the Fillmore West. They were showing the original 1933 version of the movie *King Kong* at the shows as the band took the stage, with the line in the movie, "It wasn't the airplane, it was beauty that killed the beast," and I had the idea to include that in the record. We got permission and ended up using the line in the song "Clergy."

It was a wild time in my life—it's hard even for me now to believe what it was like. Not only were they getting high all the time, they would spike people left and right with acid—meaning, get them high without them knowing it was happening. There was one guy in San Francisco who worked at Wally Heider's; they spiked his drink and he wandered off. We didn't see him for two days, and then he came back and quit.

They even got Bill Graham. Bill didn't do drugs, and he was very careful. But he loved Coca-Cola. They used a hypodermic needle to inject the LSD into his can of Coke. I don't know what happened, but six months later Bill got divorced and changed his whole life. I'm just saying . . .

Of course, they got me, too. It was in 1969 when I was doing the first Hot Tuna record, called *Hot Tuna*. It was a wonderful live blues-folk album that Jorma and Jack did together, with Will Scarlett on harmonica, without the rest of the Airplane, before the band started seriously touring for *Volunteers*.

It was Owsley who spiked me. We were recording in Berkeley, California, at a venue called the New Orleans House, and Owsley was mixing front of house. We had the Wally Heider remote truck there and I was producing. My engineer that night was Allen Zentz, who worked for RCA at the time, and later went on to start his own mastering house. I was out in the house before the show started, sitting at the bar drinking an apple juice. I must have taken my eyes off my drink because Owsley got me.

I finished my juice, and when the band was getting ready to go onstage, I went out, got in the truck, and sat down with my pad and pencil to make notes on the show. Then, all of a sudden, the truck went *whoosh!* It just expanded, and I could see that my feet were a mile and a half away. I didn't know what was happening at first. Then it happened again and I knew. I turned to Allen and said, "You're on your own," and then just sat there, whacked out, in the truck the whole night, enjoying the show. I still love that record. We had no idea how important that record would be and how well it would do.

Today, Jack and Jorma are the salt of the earth. They're both married, and they stay straight. I saw them when they got their Grammy Lifetime Achievement Award in 2016, and we talk a lot on the phone. They still travel and play together all the time.

When the Airplane started their own label, Grunt Records, I also started producing albums for Grunt. I did an album with Jack Traylor, a college teacher. In the band with Jack was Craig Chaquico, who was only sixteen years old. Jack wound up getting busted for dealing large amounts of dope and going to jail with a long sentence. But Craig, a nice kid and a really good player, especially for his age at the time, joined Jefferson Starship. Every couple of years we make contact, and it's always nice to hear from Craig who is such a talented guitar player. He went on to become a smooth jazz artist, performing New Age music and doing really well.

So, you can see, the Airplane, which is no more, generated quite a family tree of people. Like the Grateful Dead sang, it was "a long strange trip," in those days, and I'm glad I got to be a part of it.

GEORGE BENSON

I first saw George Benson play in a club in San Francisco. Tommy LiPuma and I were driving back into the city one night from the Sausalito Record Plant studios where we'd been working with Dan Hicks and the Hot Licks. We crossed the Golden Gate Bridge into San Francisco, and were driving through North Beach on the way to our hotel, when we saw "Tonight! George Benson!" on the big marquee in front of a club called Keystone Korner. We parked, bought tickets, and went in.

George was, and still is, a terrific guitar player, and it was a really good show—all instrumental. Except, at the very end of the set, George sang one song, a version of George Gershwin's "Summertime," and he did that really well, too. We didn't know him at that point, so we didn't try to go back stage and see him, we just left. But on the way back to the hotel, we talked about what a great singer he was and wondered why he wasn't singing on more songs.

About a year later, George got signed to Warner Bros., where, at the time Tommy was a staff producer. There were a lot of people interested in working with George; he'd just come off of making some good jazz records with Creed Taylor's CTI label. Bob Krasnow, who at the time was vice president of talent acquisition at Warner, had signed George to a record deal, and they were looking for a producer to work with him. Tommy was one of the producers who met with George, and during the meeting, Tommy said, "Man, you know I love the way you sing. You need to sing on at least one song on this album."

George's eyes lit up at that, because none of the other producers thought of him as a singer. They were all planning for an instrumental album because instrumentals were all they knew he'd ever done. So, when Tommy mentioned doing a song with vocals to George, that was it. He got the job.

The next thing I knew, we were doing a session at Capitol for what became George's *Breezin'* album, with an amazing band: Harvey Mason on drums, Phil Upchurch on guitar, Stanley Banks on bass, Ralph MacDonald on percussion, and two keyboard players who played with George all the time, Jorge Dalto and Ronnie Foster. We were knocking out tracks—a lot of them on the first take—and all sorts of people were coming by to hang out, because the sessions were so much fun and everything sounded so good.

At one point, Tommy surprised me and said, "Now, we're going to do a take of 'This Masquerade,' and we'll have George put a vocal on it." Well, that was okay, except that I had set everybody up in a semicircle around the drummer. There were some gobos in place to isolate the drums a bit, but there was nothing in place to provide any separation for a vocal. I just hadn't planned for that.

The band was ready to go, so I looked around, saw one of those cheap gray Electro-Voice 666 microphones, grabbed it, and put it in front of George. I was thinking it would just be a guide vocal, and that we'd overdub the real vocal later when everybody else was done and we had time to try out some mics and get a good vocal sound.

Well, as it ended up, I eventually got that mic from Capitol and gave it to the Grammy Museum, because George nailed it on the first take. The band played the track down and he sang it all live while he was playing guitar. It was also the first time down for the band to play "This Masquerade," and he just plain killed the vocal. We didn't have to do it over. Which just goes

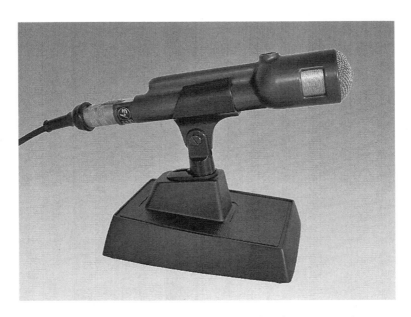

Electro-Voice 666. *(Photograph courtesy of Prof. S. O. Coutant)*

to show, it is possible to get a great vocal with a cheap, ninety-nine-dollar mic. When the next album came around, I tried to put a better vocal mic on George, but he wanted the same old 666. He was superstitious, and so we were stuck with it for that second record we did together, too.

When we finished the *Breezin'* recordings, we had a total of eight songs. Six of the songs were done on the first take. Only six songs out of the eight made it to the album, and I'm not sure anymore which were first takes, except for "This Masquerade." That one I'm sure of.

That project generated some other crazy stories. We cut all the tracks at Capitol, running the tape machine, as we usually did, at 30 ips (inches per second). When the tracks were done, Tommy and I took the tapes and went to Munich, Germany, where we were going to have Claus Ogerman add the strings. The morning after we got to Munich, we met with Claus, and then we went to a gorgeous, big studio where there was a symphony orchestra playing. They were the same musicians we were going to have playing on our record that night. They sounded amazing and they were using all these great microphones and a Neumann console. The tape machine, I didn't recognize. But I did notice that it was running at a slow speed, so I took a closer look, and saw that it was only able to record at 7 1/2 or 15 ips. Well, our tapes were at 30, so that wasn't going to work. I told Tommy, and he talked to Claus. They didn't know what to do, but they started making phone calls.

They tried to get a different motor for the tape machine that would let it run at 30, or to find some other way to make it work, but they had no luck. Nobody had a solution. But God bless Claus—he knew producer Giorgio Moroder, who also had a studio in Munich. He called Giorgio and asked, "What are you doing?" Giorgio replied, "Not much, just some editing," and Claus told him, "Good. At eight o'clock tonight, we've got an orchestra coming over."

As it turned out, Giorgio's studio was nothing like the beautiful studio we'd originally booked. It was small, and the ceiling was so low the violinists' bows could bump into it. Really, that's how cramped it was. And I had three arco basses set up in the corner, meaning, the bassists would be bowing, too. It was really tight quarters.

There was a twenty-four-track tape machine, and it ran at 30 ips. But it only had one meter, with a switch so that you could change the meter to monitor the track you wanted to look at. To see track 1, you had to switch to track 1, and then you had to switch again to see what was going on with track 2. Twenty-four tracks, one meter, and a switch. Needless to say, the session didn't go very quickly.

Ultimately, it got to be four a.m., and we were still working. The orchestra had been playing all day, and they were exhausted. Things were not going well at all. We'd planned to get everything done in one day, but it was clear that wasn't going to happen, and we decided we were done. At four thirty a.m., we finally quit, and decided to find some other way to get the rest of the strings recorded.

The next day was a Tuesday, and Tommy called around and managed to book time at CTS Studios in England, which was located next to Wembley Stadium in northwest London. But the only day they could fit us in was Sunday. When Tommy hung up the phone, he looked at me and said, "You ever been to Paris?"

"No."

"Wanna go?"

And that's what we did. We flew to Paris, hired a driver, and pretty much stayed up for four days, partying. Neither Tommy nor I spoke French, so we brought the driver with us into all the restaurants we went to so he could translate. At night, we'd go back to the hotel and drink Champagne. We kept the tapes in our hotel room, and on the weekend, we flew to London to do the rest of the orchestra songs. CTS was a beautiful room, and we were happy with the results we got there. So, we'd put orchestra on six songs; three in Munich, and three at CTS.

On the way home from London, the plane was getting ready to land in Los Angeles when they closed the airport and diverted us to, of all places, Las Vegas. The airline was putting us up for the night in a hotel, but we still had the tapes with us and we decided that, in Vegas, we didn't want to take the tapes with us to the hotel.

Truth be told, Tommy and I were juicing pretty heavy in those days. When we were traveling together, we'd generally get to the airport in the morning and have a couple of Bloody Marys, and then we'd have a couple more on the plane. When we'd get to our destination, we'd have lunch with a bottle of wine, and it went on from there. We were young and definitely foolish. But we weren't completely irresponsible, especially about master tapes. Knowing we would be partying in Vegas, we decided the tapes would be safer locked up somewhere other than with us. So, when we got off the plane, we put the tapes in a locker at the airport, then went to the hotel, checked in, and went down to the bar—which of course had slot machines.

I hit the jackpot on a quarter machine, and we put the quarters on the bar and drank them all away. It was a long night. We were supposed to have a wakeup call at eight a.m., but we either didn't get it, or we slept through it—I don't recall. Either way, we ended up missing our flight. We had to scuffle to make the next plane, but when we got to the airport, fifteen minutes before departure, we discovered that our gate was at the opposite end of the airport from the locker with the tapes. So, there we were, Tommy and me, totally hung over and running, first to the locker, where we grabbed the tapes, and then all the way back through the airport to our plane. But we made it.

I mixed the album at Capitol and didn't really think any more about it once we were done. But all of a sudden, the single "This Masquerade" became a huge hit, and *Breezin'*, the album, was a big hit, too. Of course, Tommy and I were thrilled.

Then, a few months later, we were working together at Capitol and someone came into the studio and said to me, "Do you know that you just got a Grammy nomination for engineering the *Breezin'* album? I started laughing and said, "Really? Has anybody listened to the strings?" Because we'd kept the strings we did in Munich on three of the songs, and they were, well, what can I say? There was no air in that room. It was not a great recording.

But that didn't seem to matter. People loved the recording and the album won, I think, four Grammys. You know, I'd have a lot more Grammys than I do now if they'd been giving Grammys to engineers in the album categories back in those days. *Toto IV,* Steely Dan's *Aja,* those records, and others I worked on, won Grammys. But back then, the engineers weren't eligible to win. Things change, and I'm very grateful for all of the Grammys I do have, but I'm just saying . . .

It's wonderful, though, that *Breezin'* won. George is a true artist and he deserved it. He's also fun to work with and he tells great stories. It's always a pleasure to work with him. But mostly, the pleasure of working with George is that his talent and musicianship never fail to blow me away. When we were recording, and I was out in the studio talking to him, he always had his guitar in his hands and he'd be noodling. Sometimes, I'd stop dead, in the middle of a sentence, because he'd just played something that was so fantastic, I'd have to say, "What the heck was that?" It was so easy for him. "Ahh, I'm just fooling around," is what he'd answer. He's a tremendous musician, and, a great, great singer.

George always treated me well and we got along. What did I learn from him? He's another one where you have to be on your toes. A lot of the time he gets it on the first take, so you always want to have him sounding good right away.

Another thing I learned was, you have to keep your eye on him. I was mixing a big band project for him once at Power Station in New York City. I was sitting at the console mixing away, and all of a sudden, the sound on the guitar started changing. I couldn't figure it out and it was driving me crazy. Then I turned around and saw that George was behind me, with his hands on the equalizer on the back wall that we were using on the guitar. He was over there changing the sound around, trying to find something he liked, while I was in the middle of a mix. Meanwhile, I was sitting there thinking I was losing my mind. But no, it was just George, doing his thing.

Also, George is one of the most amazing Ping-Pong players I've ever been around. He's a champion. We were always throwing guys against him who were really good, but he was better. Nobody could beat him.

Something else I really like about George is that he's punctual and always prepared. We did a lot of work together in New York where we used musicians who played in major bands, but who also did studio sessions, and some of them were notorious for always showing up late to the studio. George was always on time, and usually the first one there, so he really bristled if people were late. He knew that it was his money that was being wasted and that really affected him.

I always look forward to working with George. Going into a session with him, you know you are going to hear some fabulous music. He sings well, he plays his butt off, and the musicians love playing with him.

TOTO

One of the main things I learned from working with Toto was: have fun making records. It was always a ball to be in the studio with those guys. It was silly sometimes, stupid sometimes, but it was always enjoyable. The music was good, the players—the band members, of course, and the others who sat in, too—were all terrific musicians and in-demand session players and it was always a good time. I think that's one of the reasons *Toto IV* came out so well; it was a fun project for everybody.

I recorded six of the tracks at Sunset Sound's Studio 2, including the three songs that went top ten: "Rosanna," "I Won't Hold You Back," and "Africa." Later, we moved to, I think, Studio 1 for overdubs, where at times we had three twenty-four-track machines linked together and we overdubbed horns, vocals, keyboards, and some of the guitar solos.

It was Toto's final album with the original lineup, with David Paich on keyboards and lead and backing vocals. Steve Lukather was on guitar, lead and backing vocals, as was Bobby Kimball. Jeff Porcaro played drums and percussion, Steve Porcaro was on keyboards that were overdubbed later, and also lead vocals for "It's a Feeling." David Hungate was on bass. Lenny Castro was also there on percussion for the tracking.

All the basic tracks I cut were done live, with everybody in the room. The way I set up for them was: Jeff Porcaro's drums were in the studio next to the wall. Right next to him was Lenny on percussion. David, the bass player, was on the other side of Jeff, and the three of them were facing David Paich, who was on keyboards on the other side of the room. Lukather was next to Paich, and we had boxed his guitar amp in with gobos against the wall that was in front of the control room.

They all sat close together, and they could all both see and talk to one another. There were no iso booths. I didn't use them, but the studio didn't have any anyway. Not a lot of studios did then.

The day we started, I had a session earlier in the day at nearby Hollywood Sound, recording a singer that Stuart Levine was producing. I left there to go over to Sunset Sound, where we set up quickly and got right into recording. I remember, at one point, David Paich said, "When is Al going to get sounds?" But I was already done with that; we were ready to record. The first track we did was "Rosanna," and the master was the second take, with the improvised piano solo by David Paich on the way out.

Arranger Jerry Hey did almost all of the horn charts and he, of course, is wonderful. He's a marvelous player and a great arranger, an extraordinary talent. Small four- or five-piece horn sections are his specialty; his voicings are amazing and there's nobody like him. He had a group of players he used all the time; he knew them well and what he could get out of each of them musically, so he could tailor his writing for their capabilities. Jerry was very special, and still is. You have to be on your toes working with him; he works very fast and that keeps the energy high. This was before Pro Tools, of course, and we were doubling things and going back and forth between different tracks with different parts on the fly. Jerry knows exactly what he wants to do and what it should sound like. You should definitely check out the *Toto IV* horn arrangements; they're some of the best ever.

The band itself was producing on *Toto IV*, and as I recall, they were working on parts and sounds all the time while we were tracking. David mostly arranged the background vocals, but except for that, each person pretty much took lead on producing their own tunes—the ones they had written. And each musician also took control of his own parts and sounds. So, if Luke was doing a guitar solo, when he was happy with the solo, it was done.

For "Africa," Jeff and Lenny went out in the studio and played a drum and percussion groove. Jeff picked the two bars that he liked the best, and that became the drum track for the song. We had to loop it, and in those days we didn't have a digital way to do that. We had to record the two bars of drums to a 2-track and then cut together a tape loop. Then we'd let the loop play over and over and record that back to the multitrack. Because the distance between the tape reels on the 2-track wasn't long enough to create a two-bar loop, we also had to drape the tape around a mic stand set a few feet away. The loop went from the left reel on the tape machine, around the mic stand, and then back to the right reel of the tape machine. That's how we did it in those days.

With Toto, everybody got along well and they were always nice guys to be around. There were five of them in the band, and they each had a different personality, but they were all easy to work with. The best part is we're all still good friends! (See Appendix B for a diagram of the Toto IV sessions.)

AL JARREAU

Here's a story from *We Got By*, the first album I did with Al Jarreau.

Sometime in 1975, I got a call from a guy named Patrick Rains; my attorney, Al Schlesinger, had given him my name and number. Pat told me that he was managing a singer named Al Jarreau, and asked if I would come out to see him perform. I said, "Sure," and a few nights later I met Pat at the club where Al was playing, a little place called the Bla-Bla Café on Ventura Boulevard in Studio City. It was just Al, doing his gymnastic vocal things, and a piano player named Tom Canning on electric piano. They did a set, and I was just sitting there with my jaw hanging open pretty much all the way through, thinking, "This guy's amazing."

When the set was over, Pat told me that he had previously brought a few people by to see the show, who all liked it but said that they didn't know what to do with Al. They just couldn't figure out, musically, where he would fit in. When Pat told me that, I said, "Well, if it was up to me, I wouldn't do anything with him. I'd just let him do what he already does. He's that great."

A few weeks later, we put a rhythm section together for Al and he got a gig opening at the Troubadour, which was a pretty big deal. I told Tommy LiPuma about Al, and Tommy, who was on staff at Warner Bros. at the time, got people from Warner—including Mo Ostin, who was head of the company—to come out to see him. Well, it was an incredible show, they loved it, and Warner Bros. ended up signing Al to a deal on its Reprise label.

So now, Al's signed, and I'm going to produce and engineer his record. We went into a studio called Sound Labs, which was owned by engineer Armin Steiner, with Al and the rhythm section: Tom Canning on keyboards, Arthur Adams on guitar, Joe Carrero on drums and Paul Stallworth on bass.

The first song we cut was called "Spirit." We did two or three takes, and the musicians were all totally nailing it. I brought the band into the control room to listen to a playback of the best take, and everybody loved it. All of us were digging it. But then, while we were still listening, the control room door opened, and a woman walked in. It was Al's girlfriend Susan, who later became his wife. She and Al started talking in the back of the room, and when we finished the playback, Al came over to me and said, "Susan doesn't think this is a good take."

I said, "Really?" and then I rewound the 2-inch tape, picked up the phone, and called my home. When my wife at the time answered, I played the song over the phone for her. When it finished, I asked her, "How'd you like that?" And she said, "Oh, man, it's killer!"

I turned around and said to Al, "Well, my wife thinks it's killer." He looked at me, staring, really, for a long minute, and then all of a sudden, he broke into a big smile. See, I knew I had to nip that in the bud right away. I was the producer. I had an album to make, and I couldn't have a girlfriend jumping in on the very first song and deciding what was the right take. I had to stop it, and at the time, that seemed like the best way to do it. And Al, of course was a very smart guy; he got it. He understood right away.

We did four albums together in that first batch of music, from 1975 to 1978, and I also did some more records with Al later on. Out of those first four, Tommy LiPuma coproduced two of them with me, the second and the third. The first was *We Got By*; the second, which Tommy coproduced, was *Glow;* the third was the live double album *Look to the Rainbow: Live in Europe*, which Tommy and I did together, and then the fourth was *All Fly Home*, which I produced with Hank Cicalo engineering.

My other funny story is about *All Fly Home.* We'd almost finished the album; everything was done except for two songs that needed solos. Al asked me what I thought about getting trumpeter Freddie Hubbard to do the solos. I thought it was a fabulous idea.

We had $2000 left in the budget, so I called Freddie and told him I was doing an album with Al Jarreau, we thought he'd be perfect for two of the songs, and would he come down to the studio and play the solos?

Freddie said, "Great, how much can you pay me?" I asked, "How much do you want?" He said, Two thousand dollars," and I replied, "You got it!"

All of a sudden, there was dead silence for about fifteen seconds, and then he said, "Al, did I sell myself short?" I just laughed and said, "No, you hit it right on the head!" But you see, when I answered so quickly, Freddie thought he'd priced himself too cheap.

What a phenomenal artist Al was. Tommy and I did *Look to the Rainbow* over two months in Europe with the Rolling Stones' remote truck. I was the engineer, and it was so exciting. The crowds loved Al; you can hear them going crazy on the record. You need to listen to Al's rendition of "Take Five" on that album. Abraham Laboriel Sr. was on bass, Tom Canning on keyboards, Joe Carrero on drums, and Lynn Blessing played vibes. Overall, it's just a great, great record. It has been one of the privileges in my life to be able to have done so many records with someone as artistic and soulful as Al Jarreau.

PAUL HORN

I have worked with flautist Paul Horn quite a lot, and with Paul, there's always something unusual going on. When I was producing his album *Cycle* at RCA on Sunset and Vine, for one session we had four bagpipes. And this was a jazz record! I would never do that again. The sound is crazy. First, they have to blow up the instrument to inflate it, then the sound starts, and then it stays, and stays. It doesn't go away! When the player stops breathing, there is still air in the bag and the sound keeps going. It drove me nuts. Paul always had some wild ideas.

I also produced an album for him that was the Catholic Mass performed in jazz form by a quintet with orchestra and choir. We hired Lalo Schifrin, the composer of the music for the TV show *Mission Impossible*, to compose, arrange, and conduct, and it was called *Jazz Suite on the Mass Texts*. We brought in the New York priest Father Norman J. O'Connor, nicknamed the "Jazz Priest," who had his own radio shows and produced concerts, to write the liner notes. That album won two Grammys.

Paul had become famous with the recordings that he did at the Taj Mahal in India, *Inside* and *Inside II*. I did the second one, *Inside II*, in 1988 and it was a memorable experience. I got to meet Rajiv Gandhi, who had become the prime minister of India when the previous prime minister, his mother, Indira Gandhi, was assassinated. Paul and I had a meeting with Rajiv at two in the morning; that's when our appointment was. I don't know how Rajiv did it. He had appointments until four in the morning and then he'd start again at nine.

When we met with him, we were trying to get permission to go back into the Taj Mahal to record. He asked me what kind of equipment I would be using, and I told him I just had a couple of microphones and a new kind of small stereo recorder that was called a DAT (digital audio tape) machine. Rajiv really surprised me when he said, "Oh, I have one of those." DATs had just come out, and they were made mostly by Japanese manufacturers, so I was curious about how he'd gotten one. He said, "The Japanese contingent came over and gave it to me as a gift." So, he had a DAT and was actually recording things with it. He was an airplane pilot as well; an amazing man, who himself was assassinated just three years after we made the recording. It was a very troubled time in India.

After the meeting, we got our approval to do the project and we were allowed into the Taj Mahal, where we set up our mics on stands, very close to where Paul would be positioned. We weren't allowed to hang anything, and we had to wait to go to work until nightfall when the tourists had all left. We also had to wait for the pigeons. The Taj Mahal is open to the sky, you know, and large groups of pigeons nest up at the top. We had to wait for them to get settled in for the night and for all the cooing to stop. When it got dark and the pigeons went to sleep, we started recording.

We didn't wake the pigeons; mostly they slept all night. But the echo time in the Taj Mahal is about fifteen and a half seconds long—it's like a natural Echoplex. And every so often, in the middle of a song, we'd hear *Splat! splat, splat, splat, splat, splat*, when a pigeon had taken a poop. You'd hear the splat in the echo—all over the building. We'd have to stop and wait for it to die down, and then do another take.[2]

It was just Paul playing that night, along with a cantor—a building sentry, actually, who sang the Hindi chants and, by a wonderful coincidence, had also been there and sang with Paul when he made his first Taj Mahal recording in 1968. Paul had a bunch of different kinds of flutes with him—I remember particularly a Chinese wooden one, and he also played soprano saxophone on this album. It was all improvisation.

No one interrupted us once we were recording, but we did have soldiers from the army stationed outside, watching to make sure no one came in while we were recording. We worked until two in the morning, and then came back and did it again for a second night. That was definitely a unique and wonderful experience.

PHIL RAMONE

Something Phil was known for throughout his career was that he always wanted to use new technology. For example, he'd produced the first commercially released digital compact disc; it was Billy Joel's album *52nd Street*. Phil was always on top of the latest gear, and if something interesting came out, he wanted to try it. Even if he, himself, couldn't figure out how it worked he'd just say, "I want to use this; you guys figure it out." And then, a lot of the time, he'd leave! Then it was on us engineers, the maintenance crew, and everybody else to do just that—figure it out.

Phil was also always on top of who the great new artists were, sometimes long before anybody else was, and he had the respect of so many established artists—Paul Simon, Billy Joel, Burt Bacharach, Carly Simon—they all loved him. They were comfortable putting themselves in his hands. They knew he was meticulous. He didn't let even little things go by, but it was always about what was best for the artist. If there was an easy way to do things, but the artist wasn't going to shine as much, that was out. We took the hard way. Like installing and learning the EDNet system on the Frank Sinatra *Duets* record for long-distance collaboration. It was a technology that was brand new in 1993, and we were among the first to use it. It was going to make it easier on the artists to record in their own environments, wherever that might be, rather than traveling to us in New York—so, no matter how complicated it was to install and use, that's what we did.

Phil had an extraordinary sensibility of what was the right thing to do for a record. We did an album together with Shelby Lynne called *Just a Little Lovin'*, one of my favorites because it's just Shelby and the rhythm section and it sounds fabulous. We'd planned to add strings and maybe horns—we had it all sketched out in advance. Shelby sang the songs live with the rhythm section, and that part was done in a week. At the end of the week, we listened back to everything and Phil said, "This record is done."

He scrapped everything we'd been planning to add. He loved the fact that there was so much space, and how good everything sounded and how great she sang. He'd had string and horn arrangements done up and everything was ready to go, but we didn't use them. Another producer might have said, "Well, I paid for the arrangements, let's at least try this." But not Phil. He said, "It's done. We don't need them. This record sounds great the way it is." And he was right. He had great taste.

Phil was also very musical. He'd been a child prodigy violinist; at a very young age he'd played for the Queen of England. He was also a great engineer in his own right; he had won a Best Engineered Recording Grammy for the work he'd done on *Getz/Gilberto* album—the one with "Girl from Ipanema." He also had great studio smarts. He knew how to talk to people and how to make them feel good. He always had stories to tell that made everybody feel at ease and relaxed; from the assistants and runners on up, everybody would be on the edge of their seats listening. A lot of times we'd stay two or three hours after a session was done, just hanging out. He'd tell a story, then I'd tell one. It went on like that and everybody would stay late with us and listen. He made it fun.

He also made you feel as if he cared about you personally. But it was always about the artist first, making sure they were comfortable, and that the songs were right for them. He never forced them to sing songs they weren't comfortable with. Also, he was always listening. Even if you didn't realize it, he was tuned into what was going on. During a session, he might be in the control room telling a story, then, all of a sudden, he'd hear something, stop, and say, "We've got to fix that." Because, no matter what else was going on, part of him was always listening.

The Frank Sinatra *Duets* record was the start of Phil and I working together, and he often called me after that to do dates with him. I miss him a lot. I've been blessed all my life to work with so many greats, people like Tommy LiPuma, David Foster, Tommy Dowd, and Phil; real music men who made great records, and Phil was one of the best. He was a producer's producer, one of the few like that, and it doesn't get much better. He knew all the musicians, and he knew how to handle people and make them comfortable. Working with him was a great life learning experience.

FRANK SINATRA

I can sum up what I learned from Frank in two words: *be prepared*. With Frank, you only got one chance. You couldn't say, "Gee, Frank, sorry, the mic went bad." It was one chance and you'd better be on your toes.

I'd seen him live when I was a kid in New York, I'd seen him live when I was an adult, I'd seen him do his show in Vegas. He was one of my idols when I was a kid. I was a huge fan and I think he was probably the best singer that ever lived. I don't think anybody will even come close to him. In his time, at his peak, he was simply the best, with his phrasing, his understanding of songs, and the way every word was clear as a bell. He had beautiful articulation. Every word had a *g* on the end of it when it was supposed to—he was impeccable. Listen carefully to him and you'll hear what I mean.

I worked with Frank on his two *Duets* albums, starting in 1993. How it came about, was that Phil Ramone and I had been long-time friends. We used to hang out together and party. But the first time I actually worked with him was on the first Frank Sinatra *Duets* album. It's funny, really. I did an interview in a magazine where they asked me if I had any regrets in my career. I answered that I had one regret: that I hadn't worked with Frank Sinatra.

Three weeks later, I got the call from Phil Ramone. That happened with Paul McCartney, too; somebody asked me who I hadn't worked with that I'd like to, I said, "Paul," and shortly after that it happened—I did a record with Paul! Bob Dylan, too; I've pretty much gotten my bucket list done now.

For the first *Duets* album, Phil was set to be the producer. And even though we were great friends, I know that before he hired me to work with him on it, he asked around. "Who's the best engineer that also can stand up to that kind of pressure?" And everybody told him, "Al."

That's why I got the job; it was really a pressure gig. Frank walked in, and snap! When he was ready to sing, you had better be ready also. He sang it down one time and you couldn't have a problem. You had to be prepared. And you had to know what you were doing. Because he did. He knew exactly what he was doing and expected everybody involved to be operating on the same principle.

Phil had worked with Frank before, so he knew what to expect. What we didn't know though, was that *Duets* would end up being Frank's biggest-selling record. It sold over two million copies, so it was a very big deal for him. When we made that record, he hadn't recorded anything in a very long time, and everyone was worried about whether he was going to be able to do it or not. Fortunately, it was a duets record, so, for sections that maybe weren't as good as they could be from Frank, we were able to eliminate his vocal and put the guest artists in those spots.

My wife, Lisa, and I had just gotten married and I was busy and enjoying life when I got the call from Phil. "Hey Al, how are you doing?" Then he gave me some dates, over about three weeks, and asked me if I was available. I said, "Yeah, I'm cool for that," and he said, "Great, mark it down. What do you charge?" I told him, and I could tell it took him aback. It kind of stopped him for a second, but he didn't say anything about it.

We kept chatting for a while, everything was good with both of us, and we were getting ready to hang up, so I said, "By the way, who's the artist?" And he answered, "Frank Sinatra." I started to laugh and said "Phil, if you had told me that in front, I would have done it for nothing!" And he said, "Al, if you would have asked me for more, I would have given it to you." That was Phil. He was so cool, and so quick with his reply.

Our working relationship started with that phone call, and ultimately, for the *Duets* album, we wound up in New York doing things like getting Charles Aznavour to sing his part of the duet in Paris while we were playing back the track and recording him in New York at Hit Factory studios. *Duets* was the first major record to use EDNet. The technology was brand new at the time, and it allowed us to do long-distance recording in real time. Like I said, with technology, Phil was always ahead, and using EDNet on this project was his idea.

But, for the start of the album, we were at Capitol, where we were using both Studios A and B. Phil asked me how I was going to set up and I told him we'd put the big band in A with the rhythm section, and in B we'd have the strings—violins, viola, cellos, and harp. Phil also had a vocal booth built in studio A. It was good sized, and it actually had a duct running air-conditioning to it. In the booth, we had a little table set up with a bottle of Jack Daniels, a carton of Camel cigarettes, and bunch of Tootsie Rolls—Frank liked Tootsie Rolls.

Well, the first night, Frank didn't show up. Everybody was there, all the musicians were set up and ready to go, and we got the call, "He's not coming today; he's not feeling well." We were actually fine that night when we heard he wasn't coming, because we were able to spend the session running down all the songs and getting sounds. We used the time well.

The next night, Frank came in. All his sessions were at night. He didn't sing during the day, and we had an eight p.m. start time. When he came in on the second night, he asked me where I wanted him to be. I was standing out in the studio with him at the time, so I showed him the vocal booth. He looked at it and said, "I'm not going in there." I said, "Okay, where do you want to be?" And his answer was, "How about right here in front of the band?"

I said, "All right." Because at that point, where Frank sang wasn't my problem. If he didn't want to sing in the booth, it was Phil Ramone's problem and he was going to have to deal with it. I wasn't going to say to Frank, "Oh, no, you can't be standing out there in the room." So, I told him it was fine. Also, he wanted a handheld mic, not his normal Frank Sinatra mic—the U 48 we had warmed up and ready for him. The handheld he wanted was a wireless Vega mic. He used that, and he sang for about five minutes. Then he stopped and said, "Not tonight, guys," and left. Phil was right there next to me at the console, and when I turned to look at him, he shrugged his shoulders, "Hey, what are we going to do?"

So, that was the second night, and by then we were starting to get nervous. Charles Koppelman, who was the head of EMI and Capitol at the time, kept coming by the studio to see what was going on. When Charles didn't come in, Don Rubin, his partner, did. This was a big, expensive project, and on their watch.

On the third night, again we got the band and everything ready. Frank arrived, walked in, and said hello to everyone. Of course, everybody called him Mr. Sinatra, or Mr. S. He went up to the mic stand, took the mike, the band hit it on "Come Fly with Me," and Frank started singing.

I was in the control room, with the mic level already set, and when I heard his voice come out of the speakers, it sounded great. The hair actually stood up on my arms. I turned around and Phil was sitting behind me with a giant grin on his face. Frank's manager, on the other side of Phil, was smiling, Don Rubin was in the control room with us and he was smiling. Everybody was thinking, "Wow. This is actually going to work."

And that was it. Frank sang all the songs down once—one take each. On a few of them, he stopped in the middle because he didn't like the tempo or something else and started over. But all the rest were one take, top to bottom. All of them, on that first *Duets* album, were done that way, in one night, one take each.

Because that's how it was done, when we were finished, we didn't have multiple takes to work with. What we had, we had. And Phil, being Phil, and as smart as he was, knew that if there were a couple of things that weren't right, it was okay, because we were going to be doing duets with Luther Vandross, Bono, Streisand, all sorts of great people, and we could have them sing the parts where Frank wasn't at his best.

What else can I say about that night? He was Frank Sinatra. It was a pleasure to do the session. I have a great photo of us with his arm around me, and we had dinner with him—Phil and me; Pat Williams, the arranger; and Hank Cattaneo, Frank's right-hand guy—at La Dolce Vita.

Neither Phil, nor I, nor Pat said one word at that dinner. We just listened to Frank and his team tell stories. It was definitely a night to remember. And that was it; his last session ever. He never went into the studio to record again.

For the rest of the album, Phil went around catching people all over the place. Barbra Streisand sang in California while we were in New York at Hit Factory—they had an old vintage Neve board there that we mixed on. For Barbra's song, "I've Got a Crush on You" she wanted Frank to sing something personal to her, and to use her name in it. But he didn't want to do that. It took a lot of persuasion to talk him into it, and it ended up that Hank Cattaneo got Frank to record a few lines on a DAT in his dressing room before a show, pretending he was singing to his wife, who was named Barbara. That way, it was okay with him. We took what he recorded on the DAT and Phil and I fixed it up to fit into the track.

Niko Bolas was also on our team for that record. Niko is very lovable and very good at what he does. So, it was a great combination with the three of us: me, Phil, and Niko. It was a complicated, high-pressure project, and something we were all lucky to be involved with.

(See Appendix B for a diagram of the Frank Sinatra *Duets* sessions.)

BOB DYLAN

For the recordings I made with Bob in 2016, the desire was to introduce some of the pop classics of the Great American Songbook originally sung by Frank Sinatra and others in the forties and fifties to a new audience. Bob has said he wasn't covering the songs; instead he and the band were uncovering them, and that sounds to me like what we did.

I think they were some of the best sessions I've done. We worked live, with no headphones, and we cut twenty-one tracks. Eleven of them were released on *Fallen Angels*, and the other ten on *Shadows in the Night*. We worked three weeks on those first twenty-one; then, a little over a year later, we came back and spent five weeks doing thirty more songs. We thought that second round of sessions was going to end up being three albums with ten songs each, but Bob fooled us. He put out all thirty at the same time on the album he called *Triplicate*.

It's funny how it happened, because when Jeff Rosen, Bob's manager, first called, I was booked during the dates they wanted to do the sessions. I was really disappointed, because Dylan was high on my bucket list of artists that I really wanted to work with but hadn't yet. So, when I got a call back, saying that they would move their schedule to a time when I was available, I was thrilled. Bob had heard my work, including the *Duets* album I'd recorded with Sinatra, and he wanted to do the project with me.

The five-piece band was the one Bob tours with: George Receli on drums and percussion, Tony Garnier on standup bass, Charlie Sexton on electric guitar, Donnie Herron on pedal steel, and Stu Kimball on acoustic guitar.

We went into Capitol's Studio B, and we recorded just like we did it in the old days. We had only seven microphones going through the Neve 8068 console, and the musicians were set up in a semicircle in front of Bob. Since we weren't using headphones, it was really important to make sure that everyone was comfortable and could hear each other. That's always key for a band, but without headphones it's critical.

Everything was recorded live to analog tape, to both a Studer A800 24-track and an ATR 102 2-track machine, along with a digital backup to Pro Tools at 192 kHz. We mixed to tape also, but it turned out there really wasn't a lot of mixing to be done. There was no editing, either, and for three of the songs, the 2-track we laid down ended up as the master. We used a little reverb, but no effects. It was pretty much what we did during recording that went on the album.

Bob did not want to see a lot of microphones around, so I used as few as possible and tried to hide the ones that were there as much as I could. The mics on the bass and the acoustic guitar were set a little bit away from the instruments, and down where they weren't too visible. But for the electric guitar and the pedal steel, I was able to close mike the amps because they were off to the side.

We worked for three weeks and did two three-hour sessions every day, five days a week. Tony Garnier, the bass player, is Bob's musical director; he did the chord charts, and Bob himself was the producer. Bob's producer credit on the album is Jack Frost, and he had total control over what was going on. He brought in his own music player, an old boom box, and before we got going on a track, we'd first listen to the original Frank Sinatra version of the song and talk about what we wanted to do with it.

Bob knew what he wanted to hear, and he'd make suggestions on how and what everybody played. He'd listened to the songs over and over to understand what Frank had been doing with them. By the time we started recording, he was ready to make them his own, and really, it had nothing to do with Sinatra anymore.

On a few songs, the very first take became the master. For the rest of the songs, after the first take, they'd all come into the control room and listen, and then go out, make some changes, and play it again. I'd ask them for a little more or less volume from their instruments in some places so that I could have them adjust that themselves out in the studio. For guitar solos, Charlie just played a little louder. Usually I'm riding faders, but for this record I wanted all the dynamics to come from the band and be natural. I rode faders on the vocals, but for the rest, they balanced themselves in the room. At one point, Bob couldn't hear enough acoustic rhythm guitar, so we just moved Stu closer to him. More than ever, the setup was key, but, then that was it. It went to tape just like they played it.

Initially, I did have concerns about how it was going to go. But once everything was set up, and they'd heard the first playback, Bob was really happy. I used Capitol's Frank Sinatra mic on Bob's vocals, the Neumann U 48 that is often my go-to when I'm working there. It was set pretty far back from him, maybe ten inches, and I really believe that mic helped to give this album its air. I used the 1073 mic preamps in the Neve console on all of the mics, including Bob's vocal. The only compression I used on the entire album was on Bob's voice, just a little bit of the old mono Fairchild. Like I mostly do with vocals, I'm just using a compressor for its warmth, so I just barely tapped it. For monitoring, I also used some of my favorite Capitol chamber, number Four. When Bob heard his voice, he said that he hadn't sounded that good in forty years. He was thrilled with how he sounded, and, of course, that made me really happy.

For the drummer, I used the stereo AKG C24 as an overhead. He played pretty softly, mostly brushes on a pad, but sometimes he used sticks and he also played timpani on one song.

See Appendix B for a session diagram of Bob Dylan's *Fallen Angels*,
Shadows in the Night, and *Triplicate* sessions.

I normally would use two Neumann M 149s on the bass, but because Bob
wanted so few microphones, I used just one that I aimed at the f-hole. On the
acoustic guitar, I had an Audio-Technica 4080. I used another 4080 on the
electric guitar amp and a third 4080 on the pedal steel amp. The steel guitar
amp had its own echo, but I thought it was too much. I asked Donnie to turn
it off and I used some of my Bricasti M7 reverb instead, on both the electric
guitar and the pedal steel.

We had horns on a few of the songs; D. J. Harper arranged the charts for
them. We put the horn players in an iso booth, but we left the doors open so
that the sound could leak out into the main room and Bob could hear them.
Mostly, the horns were picked up by the Neumann M 49 ambience mic that
I had set up in omni, right in the middle of the band and close to Bob and
his vocal mic. I did have some close mics on the horns, a Royer 122 on the
trombones, a Neumann U 67 on the trumpets, and a Neumann M 149 on
the French horn. But we didn't use very much of the close mics. Most of the
horn sound ended up coming from the leakage into the room.

At the end of each session, we listened back to the final takes and Bob
decided which take of each song he liked best. He wasn't interested in mixing; he said he loved the way the rough mixes sounded. We did spend a little
time doing some touchups on some of the songs, just rebalancing a bit, but a
lot of the time he ended up preferring the original rough mix.

When we started, I honestly wasn't sure whether Bob would be able to
sing these kinds of songs. But I got goosebumps the minute I heard his voice
coming through the speakers. He loves these songs, and he put his heart into

them. I think that's why the record did so well. After we finished, I got a call from Diana Krall. Bob's manager had played the album for her and she said it touched her so deeply that it made her cry. Elvis Costello and T Bone Burnett both also called to say how much they loved the record. You can imagine how good that made me feel.

TOMMY LIPUMA

Tommy LiPuma passed away while I was putting this book together. We'd just finished doing Diana Krall's *Turn Up the Quiet* record together when he left us. Tommy and I were friends for more than fifty-five years. We did 111 records together, and I think the most important thing I learned from him was that it's all about the music. (See Appendix B for a diagram of the Diana Krall's *Turn Up the Quiet* sessions.)

The way Tommy went about concentrating on the songs and the music was something special; you could say he was a total producer. Number one, he was a musician. He wasn't technically good at things, but he had great ears and, he had a great demeanor. He knew how to pull performances out of artists. That's a big part of a producer's job, and Tommy always did it in such a nice way; it was like watching a flower opening up.

I never, ever—and I can't say this about a lot of people—saw Tommy get angry on a session. He never showed that he was upset in front of people. If someone did something he didn't like, he'd always take that person aside and tell him or her about it. He'd get it out in the open that way, and then, that was it. He was done, and it was back to making records.

The other thing Tommy did—and a few other producers took a hint from him on this, and started doing it—was that he didn't stay in the control room. He sat out in the studio with the musicians. He'd be out there right in front of them, with his headphones and sheet music. That meant he could make things happen right then and there in the room. Rather than having to hit the talkback button, talk, then release it to hear what the person outside was saying, then push the button again to reply, they were all together. It made communication so much easier.

Tommy always had so much faith and trust in me. He knew that I'd get the sound right, and so he never worried about it. He just focused on what was happening out in the studio. When he was working, he became part of the band. But he also had the perspective of a great producer and saw the big picture.

He had been a good saxophone player when he was younger, so he had musical chops and he had good ears for pitch and tempo. He was from Cleveland. His father was a barber who wanted his son to be able to earn a living, so Tommy learned to be a barber, too. But, being Tommy, he became friends with a guy in the music business. That guy brought other guys in the music business to the barbershop to get their hair cut and Tommy would get to meet them.

Meanwhile, Tommy was also still playing saxophone around Cleveland with Nick and Frank DeCaro, both of whom also went on to work in the music business in Los Angeles, but who at the time were gigging playing accordion and guitar. The three of them would do gigs on the boats on Lake Erie, and eventually, someone they played for offered Tommy a job at a music company. Boxing up records, I think the job was. From there, he got into promoting records, and when I met him he was working for a music publisher. It was when I was a staff producer for RCA, and he would bring me songs. That's how we met.

Ultimately, Tommy started producing, too, and he had a big hit as a producer with "Guantanamera," by the Sandpipers. In the song, there's some dialogue that starts out, "And the words mean . . ." That's Tommy speaking. Bruce Botnick was the engineer. Tommy had tried out a few people speaking the lines, but Bruce recorded Tommy when he was out there showing the others how to say the words, and that's what they used for the record.

Since Tommy was a sax player, he could read music, and once he started producing, the more he produced, the more he learned. He was one of those people who put everything he learned back into his work. He also had great taste in songs. He'd hear songs that had been written or recorded by someone and he'd remember them, thinking that someday he'd use them for someone else.

Leon Russell was the writer of the song "This Masquerade." Tommy heard it, liked it, and played it for George Benson. "Breezin'," the title song of the album that "This Masquerade" is on, was written by Bobby Womack. That was another song Tommy found and brought to George. Tommy also brought Bobby Womack in to play guitar on the recording. When we did *The Way We Were* with Barbra Streisand, he picked out the songs with Barbra, songs about lovers being at war with each other. He just had the knack—it came naturally to him.

In the studio, Tommy always worked really easily with the arrangers on changing parts around. It was fun to watch him do that, because a lot of arrangers put out the vibe of "Don't mess with my chart!" But they let Tommy make suggestions. Everybody respected him.

He also knew how to make sessions fun. We'd be working on a project, and of course, as is my habit, I'd always arrive way early. An hour before the session, the phone would ring, I'd pick it up and it would be Tommy asking, "What are we having for lunch?" He wanted to get the lunch order in, so we had that to look forward to. Or we'd be working and working all day, and he'd stop in the middle of something we were doing and say, "Okay, where do you want to go for dinner?" It was about the music—and the food, too. The really important things.

Tommy's house, before he married his wife, Gill, was a party house. He had a great apartment on Hollywood Boulevard that he shared with the disc jockey Johnny Hayes and we all used to spend time there. Later, he bought a house in the Valley, and when I finished working at night, I'd drive by. If the lights were on, I'd park and go in, because there would always be something going on. Randy Newman was often there; for a while, while he was writing the *Redneck* album, he'd play the songs he was working on for us on the piano. Lenny Waronker, the president of Warner Bros. Records, would be there. Tommy had a pool table, and Dan Hicks would be there playing pool. It was a hangout, and a lot of fun.

We were friends for all those years and we were closer than brothers. We never had a big blowout. A couple of misunderstandings, maybe, but if I was angry with him, he'd always apologize. If he was angry with me, I'd apologize.

One time we were in Switzerland working with Al Jarreau and I was co-producing. We took a big group out to dinner, and when it came time to pay the tab, I picked it up. Well, Tommy got really mad because he wanted to pay. I got a call from him later and he said, "Let's have breakfast in the morning; we need to talk."

I knew what it was about, so when we met in the morning, the first thing I said was, "Tommy, I want to apologize for last night." That put a big grin on his face, because he knew I'd taken the wind out of his sails by apologizing before he could get into it. What we had was pretty special; it was a mutual appreciation for each other.

It also speaks to how good he was that he worked on multiple records with so many artists: Diana Krall, Natalie Cole, and George Benson, for example. You don't see that so much. And one more thing, Tommy got along really well with Miles Davis. That was difficult thing to do. They became friends, hung out together, and talked on the phone a lot. Miles didn't have many close friends, but he really liked Tommy. I'm sure that, again, it was because Tommy was all about the music, and that's what Miles cared about. Forget about the other stuff that tries to get in the way. What matters is getting the record done.

9

LIFE'S BEEN GOOD TO ME SO FAR: THE SECRETS TO MY SUCCESS

SECRET 1: YA GOTTA LOVE IT.

Something that I believe has helped me enormously in my career is that I've always had so much passion for my work. I'm totally in love with what I do; now, today, as much as I was early on. I work with musicians and artists, and I get to hang out with them—what's not to love?

But if you don't have a real, true passion for this, you should do something else. When you start out in this business, you don't make any money. The hours are nuts. All your friends are people you work with because you never get to see anybody else. I can't tell you how many times I had dates for an evening and I had to call at the last minute to break them because I was in the studio. It's a tough thing. But I don't have any complaints.

On sessions, I always enjoyed being out in the studio with the musicians, chatting and joking around, and I still do. I've become personal friends with so many of them, and we still hang out after the sessions. I think the love I have for my work shines through. It makes musicians feel good to have all that enthusiasm on their dates, and that's part of why they like to work with me.

Then, of course, when you're working a lot and doing so many dates, the odds are you're going to have hits. Early on, I did a Ray Charles/Betty Carter album, in, I think two days, the whole album—mono and 2-tracks. It was a gorgeous album—it's just called *Ray Charles and Betty Carter*—and afterward people were dying to get me to do dates for them. The great projects that I did, that were also successful, brought in more business.

I really haven't done a record that was tedious. And there have only been a couple of times in my life that I haven't wanted to go into the studio—where I was booked on something but I didn't want to go in to work.

It was rare, but it did happen. The project that I recall the most where I felt that way was with a group that was on Playboy Records. They'd had a huge hit, but then decided to get rid of their producer and hired me instead. We were working at the Village Recorder, and it was one of those sessions where we'd start later every day until finally we were going in at midnight. Unbeknownst to me at the time, they were buying cocaine and the cost of it was getting tacked onto the studio time, hidden in the invoices as some other charge. When found out, that really made me angry because, as the producer, it was my budget—I was in charge of it. But I didn't realize it at the time; I found out later.

At one point in the project we were recording the rhythm section for a song and the leader said, "You know, Al, this is kind of like a Count Basie song—do you think we can get the Count Basie orchestra?" I said, "Sure, let me try." I called Basie's manager in New York who said they'd love to do it, but that the band was in Europe for three months. So, instead, I suggested that we get someone else great who could do an arrangement that would sound like the Basie band. We didn't end up doing that, but one night, a couple of weeks later, we were in the studio at four in the morning, sitting on the floor and listening back to all of the songs.

When that particular song came on, the leader, whose name was Danny, said, "You know what's wrong with this song? You've got it sounding like a Basie song, and it's not really a Basie kind of song."

I was already not loving the sessions, but that was the final straw. My reply that night was just, "Really? Okay. Let's call it a day." I went home, and the next morning I called my attorney, Al Schlesinger, and said, "You've got to get me out of this." Which he did. We had a meeting with everybody on the project, and they paid me off. I was done, and that was that. That's one of the very few times in my career that I can remember getting up in the morning and not wanting to go into the studio. Normally I'm happy to go to work!

I'm not a religious guy, but I love what I do, and I think it's a gift from God that I can do it so well. God, or the universe, put all the right teachers in my life so that I was able learn different things from all sorts of people and put it all together. However, it came about, it's a gift that I do this.

I also love to teach, and I try to teach by example with my assistants and the people who work with me. There are assistants of mine that are now top engineers; many have become super good at what they do, and I feel blessed by that as well.

Most of the large studios with staff engineers that offered apprenticeship or intern placements are. gone now. They've closed down and there aren't many places that are able to provide those kinds of opportunities. I try to offer as much help as I can, letting kids from the recording schools come in, watch my sessions, and learn as much as possible from them.

SECRET 2: CONFIDENCE

When I was young, I never got tired of looking for new ways to do things. I knew that if we tried a new and different kind of setup for a band, and I opened up the faders and heard it wasn't working, I could get the contractor to give everybody a quick break. The contractor would tell the musicians to take five, and we'd run out to change the setup and dial it back in. Somehow, I had no fear about doing that.

Maybe my lack of fear came because I'd gained experience doing it all: country, classical, pop, big band, orchestras, and small string ensembles. I got to record everything. If it was music I didn't like, I'd still focus on getting the best sound I could out of all the instruments—even a harmonica. I never liked polka music, but if I was recording an accordion, I wanted to get the best accordion sound ever. Whatever it was, I would go in and just focus on capturing the sounds.

Some of that kind of attitude I learned from my mentors. A lot of it came from my uncle, who himself was so confident. He had a way about him that appealed to people. He was good at his work and he knew everybody; he was one of the guys. He and Bing Crosby would laugh and make fun of each other. Kate Smith, who was so famous for singing "God Bless America," would come in and visit on sessions. Orson Welles, Art Tatum, Les Paul—he was friends with everybody and everybody liked him.

He was a good guy and a talented guy who knew what he was doing, and I got that from him. When you know how good you are at something and that you can do it well, you have that confidence. There is no fear. You might be recording ninety pieces, but you know you can do it.

The largest session I ever did was in 1959 for a double album called *An Evening with Lerner and Loewe*. We did it at the Goldman scoring stage on Melrose in Hollywood, actually one of the most beautiful rooms I've ever worked in. It's not there anymore; it burned down. We were recording music from four of the Lerner and Loewe musicals that were popular at the time: *Brigadoon*, *Paint Your Wagon*, *Gigi*, and *My Fair Lady*.

Luckily, Alan Jay Lerner, the lyricist, and Frederick "Fritz" Loewe, the composer, were two of the funniest guys around. The conductor, Johnny Green, also had a great sense of humor and we did a lot of laughing on the session—which really helped.

On the session were the RCA Victor Chorale and Orchestra: eighty musicians, and a forty- or fifty-voice choir with four artists all singing live. The artists stood right next to Johnny Green: actress Jane Powell, opera singers Jan Peerce and Robert Merrill, and comedian Phil Harris, who used to be on *The Jack Benny Program*.

A lot of people would have said, "Whoa. Three guys and a female singer and all this stuff and all these people at a studio you'd never worked in before?" They might not have had the courage to do it. But, somehow, I did have the courage, and I loved it. I think what I live for is when that first playback comes, and everybody in the room says, "Oh my gosh, it sounds fabulous!"

When I had to fill in for Bob Doherty at Fulton and did my very first orchestra date, he had confidence in me and he told me, "Al, you are good enough to do this, don't worry about it, just do it." That helped, too.

Now, the more musicians there are in the studio, the happier I am. The bigger the orchestra the more the fun—because of the sound that comes out of a big orchestra. But you'd better have confidence and know how to do it or there's going to be a lot of trouble!

It's true that more you do something the more confidence you get. But also, sometimes, you just have to be able to do something you've never done before and still be confident that you are capable. You just stand up straight, hold your head up, and go in and do it.

Another thing that may have helped me was that, when I was a staff producer at RCA, every Friday night at eight p.m. there was an hour-long class for the five of us on the A&R staff, where someone had been hired to come in and coach us. He gave us lessons on how to present ourselves. He showed us how to shake hands, how to speak to a large group of people, and how it's good to try to talk about something a little humorous to start off. We learned to plant our feet, say "Hi," and put out our hand for a firm handshake. Not a sloppy, grab-the-hand-and-shake-it, but something substantial. For public speaking, we learned to be prepared, to have notes that remind us of what to talk about, and that we shouldn't get up to talk without knowing what we're going to say.

I'm not confident in everything I do, but I'm confident in interviews and I'm good on panels. For public speaking where it's just me, alone, I still get nervous. But if I have to do it, I just bring my notes and I'm okay.

SECRET 3: RESPECT

For whatever reasons, I do get a lot of respect, and when things start to get out of line I'm able to put a stop to it. How did I earn that respect? Well, for one thing I'm always prepared for what I'm going to have to do. I'm also reliable; I make sure people can count on me. I'm there early for sessions. And, I always look nice. People like that, and it inspires confidence.

I also learned about managing people by being a producer. When people would veer off from what they were supposed to be doing, I had to try to get them back in line.

Working with bands like Jefferson Airplane and Toto, groups that were used to doing their own thing all the time, I would have to pull people together when things would start to drift. It's part of the job, and, of course, there's pressure from the record companies. It's okay to have fun, but when things went too far, I'd have to steer them back on track to make sure we got the work done.

Being a staff producer at a record company made me aware of costs, overrides, and budgets. It kept me focused on what the end result should be, and I knew that if I was producing I'd have to put my foot down.

This is something that has always been very important to me: If you're hired to do a job, that's what you have to do. Having fun while doing your job is one thing, and it's okay for a minute or two. But if it detracts from where you're heading, you have to manage things and get them back on track. That's your job; that's what you're paid for. And if you don't do what you are being paid to do, you're stealing. I got that sensibility from my dad, and from my uncle.

You never want to be the bad guy, but you are, maybe, some of the time, the enforcer. It's a fine line, because if you become the bad guy, sessions can dwindle. You've got to maintain a good relationship; you can't be in the studio and be angry at the producer or the artist. Even if you're a little put out, you can't show it. You've got to keep those feelings under wraps, because it's all about the music and the artist. The artist's name goes on the front of the recording. I don't care how important you are as a producer or engineer, it's the artist's record and you have to remember that's what you are there for.

You can manage that in all sorts of ways; you just have to figure out what works. It can be as simple as, "Okay, we've had enough fun; let's get back to work." You can't go in like a marine sergeant, you have to find a more pleasant way.

Becoming friends, of course, helps with relationships in the studio. When we're done for the day, we hang out; we go hit the bars and the jazz clubs and get to know one another. For example, I haven't seen Jackson Browne in a while but we've remained friends; when we see each other, we share a big smile and a hug.

When you've put your time in, people get to know you and respect what you do. They know you're good at your work, and it's nice for them when they don't have to worry about your job. I've seen it happen, sometimes, where the artist took over because the person producing wasn't quite good enough, or maybe didn't understand what the artist wanted to accomplish. As an engineer, I've been there when that happens, and I feel for both of them—the artist and the producer. It's a problem, because if the artist has to take over, they're not able to pay attention to all the other things they should be concentrating on. And, of course, it can also be very humiliating for the producer.

It's important to establish respect, and people do it in different ways.

David Foster, for example, is extremely strong in the studio, but since he's so talented, and such a great musician, it's pretty hard to argue with him! Tommy LiPuma's way to work with artists was to have us set him up out in the studio with the musicians all around him so that he was one of them.

Every producer is different. No two are the same. They have to know how to pull performances out of the artist. It's a lot of work and a lot of details. Everyone has their own style and their own way to make it work, and I've learned from all of them.

SECRET 4: MEDITATION

Meditation is great. I actually believe that meditating may have saved my life. When I first started working with Jefferson Airplane in the sixties, everything was so nuts. I was working on two projects every day and getting only three or four hours of sleep a night. But before I went down to the studio and we started the Airplane session, I'd meditate for a full hour in my office and it would give me a renewed energy.

It was Transcendental Meditation, taught by the Maharishi Mahesh Yogi, and a lot of artists, including the Beatles and the Beach Boys, were doing it at the time. It was Paul Horn, who was a prominent disciple of the Maharishi, who taught me how to meditate and got me my mantra.

When Paul and I flew to India to record his second album at the Taj Mahal in Agra, we first made a stop in Delhi, where we got a taxi and drove about an hour and a half to see the Maharishi. Paul was an important artist, and a disciple, so we thought we'd get to see him. But instead, we sat in the office for several hours, waiting, until we were finally told, "No, Maharishi is too busy to see you today."

So, I never got to meet the Maharishi. But we spent time in New Delhi, Old Delhi, and Agra, Paul got a nice album out of the trip that did well, and I was meditating. I still do.

Like I said, I believe meditating saved my life in that stretch when I was working in the office or finding songs the first part of the day, producing Eddie Fisher in the afternoon and then back at eight o'clock that night working with Jefferson Airplane until three or four in the morning. What I would do, was, when I finished with Eddie at five, I'd go to my office. When my secretary left at five thirty p.m., I'd close the door and meditate for an hour. I'd just sit there, and it would give me the energy and the calmness to deal with the Airplane.

That's what meditation is for me. It's a calmness that gives you an energy that makes you able to face things. You don't get too upset about stuff, and it helps you pause and take time to work things out.

How I do it, is: I sit down on a chair, usually a straight-backed chair. Then, I close my eyes. I say my mantra over and over, and it just kind of goes down inside me. I've always had the same mantra. And I'll tell you a funny story about that.

It was Paul Horn who gave me my mantra. For a while in the sixties, the Maharishi's West Coast headquarters were at building that is now the Village studios in West Los Angeles, and Paul and I went to see him there. You had to bring fruit and flowers when you got your mantra, and we did. I'm not sure now how Paul got my mantra from the Maharishi, but it was Paul who whispered it in my ear. The funny thing is, I went outside afterward for less than ten minutes, and I forgot my mantra! I had to go back in and ask Paul to tell me again what it was. I felt terrible about forgetting, but then Paul told me I'd be surprised at how often it happened.

Sometime later, drummer Jeff Porcaro and I were working on a bunch of records together. He did meditation as well. We got to talking about it, and he said, "If you tell me your mantra, I'll tell you mine." Because, at that time, you were not supposed to tell anyone your mantra.

But I told him mine, which was I-Ying, I-Ying. And it turned out his was the same! We laughed and decided that when they gave out these mantras, everybody in the music business got the same one. Probably the Beatles had it, too. I've never talked to Paul McCartney about it, but I think next time I see him I'll ask him if his is the same as well.

Anyway, that's the mantra I've always used. For me, when I meditate, I get to a place where I go into a kind of void, where there is nothing. It's just black and peaceful and calm. When I come out of it, I have energy as if I had eight hours of sleep. At that time, at RCA, I was meditating an hour every night, or sometimes half an hour in the morning and a half hour at night. Back then they told you a half hour was enough. But there were times when

I'd come out of meditation and realize an hour had gone by when it seemed like only five minutes to me.

You have your mantra; you sit quietly and just repeat it over and over. Not in exactly the same way; it's like a template. But it should be loose. And you follow that mantra into a peaceful place. Other thoughts come into your head; that's a normal thing. You'll start thinking about something that happened during the day or something you have to do. But that's what you have to try to clear out; just let the thoughts go. That's how the mantra helps, because you concentrate on the mantra rather than trying to push thoughts away. Outside noise can be distracting, so you want a quiet place if you can find it.

It's interesting that so many people I know from back then who meditated, still do it today. I started with Paul Horn sometime around 1964, so I've been meditating more than fifty years. Now I meditate in the evening. Or sometimes I'll do it at Capitol. I'll take twenty minutes and go somewhere quiet. I think it is still one of the things that keeps me from getting upset in the studio. I'm generally really calm. I know anything can be fixed. If somebody makes a mistake, I tell them to let me know about it; we'll take care of it and then forget it. I can stay pretty even-tempered, and I think it's a good thing that I don't get upset and scream and yell.

Years ago, though, I did get upset. Probably between 1958 and 1964, when I got my mantra, I was pretty verbal. I'd yell at second engineers. I don't ever do that anymore; I'm pretty easy in the studio. But back then, I was very strict when mistakes were made. I thought it was inexcusable to make a mistake. But who wants to be around someone like that? It's not fun. And when you yell at someone in front of other people it hurts them.

Now, if something happens, I take the person at fault aside and say, "You've got to be careful not to do that again, because I don't want to see it again." But I also tell them, if they do make a mistake, they should tell me and then forget it. Because if they start worrying about it, they'll just make another mistake. The best way is, if you make a mistake and you can fix it, then fix it. If you can't, then just move on.

My wife, Lisa, and I still meditate every so often at home, but not as much as back then when I did it every single day. Maybe I'm just too content now. But, like I said, I'll still do it at work sometimes. If I finish a mix and I have forty-five minutes to an hour while they print stems and get set up for the next mix, I'll sit quietly and meditate. It's like having an extra battery in your arsenal.

SECRET 5: GETTING SOBER

I never drank or did drugs on sessions when I was an engineer. I admit I did smoke a joint a couple of times when I was producing at RCA. But aside from those two or three occasions, I never drank or did drugs when I was working.

But by the time I was producing and started working with Jefferson Airplane, I was well acquainted with weed. I think everyone was then. I also always liked to go out and drink when I was finished working for the day. Working with the Airplane, there were drugs everywhere, and I had access to everything. I got introduced to cocaine, then there were Quaaludes, which are illegal now. Plus, Owsley was always there, which meant acid was always there, angel dust/PCP was there, you name it. And it turned out that I liked to drink and do drugs, too. The more I drank, the more drugs I did, and that would keep me going. All my friends were into it, too. I don't think there were any of my friends at the time who weren't doing drugs.

Ultimately, it cost me. I'd already gotten my second divorce when I started to realize that I had a serious problem. But it took a long, long time to get to that place, where I knew I had to do something. What started happening was, when I was drinking, you never knew who was going to show up.

I could be the happy-go-lucky guy who was so much fun or I could be a surly jerk who would say things I'd totally regret. I'd be reminded the next day of things I'd done that I had no memory of doing. Sometimes, I'd get home and wouldn't know how I got there. Or I'd be gone for two days, and when I'd get home I wouldn't know where I'd been. I had a family, I had kids, and I started thinking, "What am I doing?"

It got to where I just didn't like myself. I didn't like looking in the mirror. I didn't like the guy that was there and I wasn't proud of who I was. It's funny, though, I always worked. Drinking and drugs didn't stop me. And people still liked me. When I wasn't that nasty guy, I was easy to get along with. I never had any problems in that regard in the studio.

I also never missed a day of work. There'd be times I'd be in the bathroom, hungover and throwing up on breaks between takes. Many times, I wouldn't get to bed at all. I'd be up all night, realize I had a session in an hour, and jump in the car and head to the studio.

But finally, I had an experience that caused a change in me. I used to have a poker game once a month with a bunch of my friends. I had a really nice poker table at my house. We'd set up, get cold cuts from a great Italian deli, and it was a fun guys' night thing. We'd laugh a lot, and everybody would be smoking weed and snorting blow. Some guys even had their own special blow that they didn't share. It was pretty wacky.

But one night, I looked up from my cards, glanced around the table and saw that everybody's mouth was moving. They were all talking at the same time! And somehow, something hit me. I looked back down at my cards and I said to myself, "I can't do this anymore."

The next day I called my friend Shelly Weiss, who was in the AA program, and I said, "Shelly, I need some help. I hear you go to these meetings. Would you let me know where the meeting is located so I can go to one?"

And he said, "No. I'll come and get you."

He didn't want to leave it up to me because he was afraid I'd change my mind and wouldn't go. He picked me up and brought me to a musician's meeting. There were about fifty people there, mostly guys, and I, literally, knew about forty of them. There were some very famous musicians and engineers, and one very well-known musician came over and said, "Hey Al, I've been saving a seat for you."

That was it. It just worked for me that first day, and I never looked back. I never had any doubts. This was where I had to be, and this was what I wanted to do. That was almost thirty years ago now.

It's the best thing I ever did for myself, and probably the best thing I ever did for my family and friends. I'm a happy guy now, and my life is good. At three years sober, I met my wife, Lisa, and we've been married more than twenty-five years. I'd never been in a relationship that long before. I always messed things up some way. With this marriage, I had a lot more understanding, and when there were problems, we worked things out. I made a commitment and I stuck to it, not like in the old days.

Now I like myself a lot. I'm a good guy and I love my wife. I'm doing good work, still. Who'd have thought I'd still be working? I'm doing all kinds of great projects.

The fact is, I don't miss drinking or drugs. Occasionally, I miss the idea of a really good glass of wine. Lisa drinks wine, and she has some great wines, so sometimes I'll smell the glass and kind of salivate. But I don't even try to taste it. I'm also a lot healthier now. I do Pilates two or three times a week. I swim in the pool thirty minutes a day. I stay in shape and I eat well. We're doing great.

Somehow, I reached a point where I could see my life going a certain way that wasn't good. I was working, although I wasn't as busy as I've been since I got sober. But I don't know how much longer I could have continued on. I would have killed myself in a car accident, or even worse, killed somebody else.

I'm proud of what I've done in getting sober, and for anybody out there who has these problems, I'd advise them to find an AA meeting and go. There is so much help there, from people who've been through exactly what you've been through. It's a fellowship, and people will go out of their way to do things that help you out.

I love that these days I see people, who were in the same boat as I was, who got sober around the same time as I did, who are healthy and happy. They're doing well, even sponsoring other people who need some help. They're successful human beings.

I still go to meetings once in a while. I used to go every day, but now, occasionally, when Lisa sees me getting a little off, she'll say to me, "You know, Al, maybe you should go to a meeting." And I'll call up one of my friends and we'll go together.

SECRET 6: MOTIVATION AND WORK ETHIC

Growing up poor, my shoes were hand-me-downs that I got from my cousins. All of my clothing was secondhand. These days I'm a sock freak and a shoe freak—I've got a lot of both. Being poor when I was young made me want to have all the luxuries—to drive a nice car and to be able to give my kids the things I didn't have.

A lot of my work ethic came from my uncle. He taught me to always be ready, and to always be prepared. To take care of equipment and make sure everything is working correctly, way before you start a session. Your work doesn't start when the session does; it starts hours before. Sometimes I'm thinking about how I'm going to do things days before a session, figuring out how I'm going to set up and what mics I'm going to use.

It also comes from things that I learned when I was really young, especially from my dad. I was always taught to treat everybody the way you wanted to be treated. I hear a lot of engineers who growl and yell at their assistants. Sometimes I did that in the past, before I started meditating, but ultimately it made me feel bad, and in my heart, I never wanted to do that kind of stuff.

Also, my father never took a day off in his life. I learned from that, and I never missed a session. My kids are the same way, so I think it is something I inherited. If my father had a cold, bursitis in his arm, however he was feeling, he still got up every day and went to work.

SECRET 7: INTEGRITY

To me, integrity is when you say you're going to do something, you do it. When you give your word, it's important to stand by it. I think that's one of the most important things in life. I never want anybody to say, "Al lied to me," or that I didn't do this, or I didn't do that.

I guess part of it is wanting people to think I'm a nice guy. Why that is important to me, I don't know. But it is. I care that people like me. Maybe it goes back to my childhood, being poor, going to school and not having things the other kids had.

I also stand up for my assistants, and for other people. I was always that way even when I was kid. In school, there was a skinny kid who wore glasses and was a little off. The other guys would pick on him all the time and I was always getting into fights to protect him. I like to speak for people who can't speak or do things for themselves. I like to help that way where I can.

SECRET 8: EFFICIENCY

I do try to be efficient. On conference calls, I'm definitely that way. Everybody is chatting, and I'll speak up, "Okay, c'mon, guys. We all have things to do; let's get this done." Because otherwise the conversation wanders off, and then the purpose of why you're there to begin with starts to disappear. Chatting a little is fine, but we've got to get down to business. Let's do what we're here to do.

Another thing is, I'm never late. I was late once because of a traffic jam. It was at RCA in 1969 or so. Fortunately, my assistant was able to get everything set up. I got there five minutes after the downbeat, while they were running through the first song. I had been in a terrible panic in the car, worrying about getting there and what was going to happen, and I didn't want that to ever happen again. So since then, I've been extra careful. I get there really early, all of the time.

SECRET 9: REINVENTION

Every project is different, and I let it dictate the direction to me. I've always tried to challenge myself by taking on different types of projects. It could be a rock band like Toto, a big band, an acoustic jazz project, or an eighty-two-piece orchestra. I did a live show with Usher and Ludacris, which was very different for me. Variety is the most exciting part. It's great to be an expert in a certain genre, but if the fashion changes, your work will dry up. I've received twenty-three Grammy statues, and they cover all sorts of different genres!

I'm always learning, and I don't think there is such a thing as a perfect-sounding record. I've made records that won Grammys and made a lot of money, but sometimes I'll hear those records two years later on the radio, and I'll think I could have done them better. I don't think I've ever made a record I was 100 percent happy with. But I don't know if too many other people would say they have, either.

SECRET 10: KEEPING PERSPECTIVE

A few years ago, I was getting ready to visit my oldest son, Al Jr., and his family, where they live in Las Vegas, when I got a call from my little grandson Peter, who was in the first grade at the time. He said, "Grandpa, when you come to visit, would you bring one of your Grammys for show-and-tell at my school? I said, "Sure."

So, I got one of my Grammys, packed it up, went to Vegas, and then, one morning, I went to school with Peter for show-and-tell in his classroom. Turns out there was a fireman up before me, and he's talking about riding in the fire trucks, fighting fires and saving buildings, all that stuff, and the kids are totally enamored. I'll tell you, that's a tough thing to follow.

But then it was my turn, and I went up to the front of the room with my Grammy, put it down on the desk and talked a little about what I do. Then, they passed the Grammy around and were asking me questions—do I know Janet Jackson, do I know Michael Jackson, all kinds of stuff. It was really fun to interact with them.

Finally, the Grammy got to a boy in the back of the room, and when he picked it up he said, "My dad has one of these, too." And I'm thinking, *what a coincidence: I'm in this classroom in Las Vegas and this kid's father is a Grammy winner as well.* So, I asked, "That's great, what did he get it for?" And he answered, "Bowling!"

I said, "Well, that's wonderful, I'm so happy for him." But I had to laugh. Leave it to a six-year-old to really make you put things in the proper perspective.

SECRET 11: KEEP THE MUSICIANS HAPPY!

Sometimes, if you're not sure where to put the mic, it's okay to ask the musicians. They may tell you, "Last time, they put the mic over here and it sounded great." So, don't be afraid to ask—especially if they come in with an instrument you've never seen before! You can try what they suggest, go out in the studio and listen, and then go back into the control room to listen some more to make sure it sounds as it should.

You always want the musicians to feel good and to know that you care about how they're feeling. I always ask them if they're comfortable, and if everything is okay. It's common sense, really. If they're happy with their sound, they're going to play better because they don't have to be worrying about how they sound.

Something I always tell people when I'm teaching is that, in the studio, the musician is your best friend. I like to greet everyone and say, "Hello. How are you doing? How are the kids?" Of course, by now, so many of them really are my friends and that helps make it fun to go to work.

It's something else I first learned from Tommy Dowd. Remember, when I started, I was a teenager working with my idols, like Charlie Parker and Dizzy Gillespie. I was in awe of them, but Tommy showed me how important it was to talk to them, to pay attention to their needs and to ensure that they were feeling good. Tommy always said, "Keep 'em happy! A happy musician will always give you the best sound."

10

SOME CLOSING THOUGHTS

___

As of January 17, 2018, I have thirty years of sobriety. I've also been married twenty-five years to my wife, Lisa, and life is good. With my previous marriages, when I was drinking, if something was going wrong, I'd just say to myself, "I don't need this." I didn't bother to take the time to deal with it. I was too wrapped up in myself; too busy working and too busy going out drinking, so I never got relationships right. Although, it's also true that for my first marriage, at age twenty-one, I was just too young. I had three kids by the time I was twenty-six, and I wasn't ready for that.

But I found that when I got sober, all that changed. Actually, a lot of my relationships changed when I got sober, with my friends as well as my family, because I was able to commit to working on them. I became much more understanding of other people and their problems and I learned how to be more of a partner and a better friend.

You can't start your life over. You can't go back to the beginning. But you can start from now, so that you make your ending better. That's what I did thirty years ago; I started to make the ending of my life better. Three years into sobriety I met Lisa, which is one of the best things that's happened to me. We love each other and we enjoy the same things. Like anyone else, we have our battles; as a matter of fact, we had one this morning. But after a while we just stopped, looked at each other, and started smiling. Then I went over and gave her a little kiss. Because a lot of making things work is about not holding a grudge. I don't stay mad at anyone. Instead, I'll get whatever it is out of the way. If somebody is doing something that's bothering me, I'll tell them about it instead of keeping it inside and letting it fester. That works.

You get it out of the way, clear it up and get back to friendship again. Besides my work, of course, my family and friends and having good relationships with them are what's most important to me.

I am so proud of my five children. All are successful adults with their own kids, and I am blessed to have great relationships with all of them. I not only love them, I respect and like them as people. I adore spending time with each of them, together with my eight grandchildren and four great-grandkids.

Lisa and I are also very interested in animals. We're making our third trip to Africa this year. The first time I went was twenty years ago and it changed my life. Seeing animals in their natural habitat—lions lying down and right next to them zebras and giraffes—you get a sense of how they basically live in harmony with one another. It's amazing, and seeing it has affected my thinking. I don't understand people who want to shoot animals for sport. I don't know what kind of joy a person can get out of killing a living being. How does it work that you want to put an animal's head up on a wall? Animals don't get angry with each other like people do; they don't murder each other or have wars. They only kill for food or to protect their young. Seeing and learning all that we have in Africa, we've become very interested in helping endangered animals, and adopting ones that need rescue. Now, in lieu of giving holiday gifts to our adult family members and friends, we donate money to the David Sheldrick Wildlife Trust for orphaned elephants and rhinos. With these gifts, everybody gets to foster an elephant or rhino and to follow along with how it is doing.

We also started adopting rescued senior dogs. We have three dogs right now and two of them are rescues: one whose owners were going to turn her back to the pound, and one who had been horribly mistreated in an illegal puppy mill. He was nine years old, beaten and scarred, and had lived his whole life in a cage. There are so many like that that need help. If we won the lottery, we'd buy some property, rescue every dog we could, and hire people to help take care of them.

Something else that's very important to us is art. Tommy LiPuma and producer Joe Wissert, who produced the Turtles, Boz Scaggs, and the J. Geils Band, among many others, are into collecting and they had originally piqued my interest. When I was at Tommy's house, I'd see the art he had and they'd talk to me about it and the artists who had created it. Then, when Lisa and I got together, we started reading up on the work and the history of artists we liked.

Eventually, Tommy and Joe introduced us to art dealers in New York. There was an auction coming up at Christie's, and we started thinking about actually getting a painting. The one we liked was by Alfred Maurer, an American modernist who was born in New York City in 1868. We bid on it, got it, and it was the most exciting thing. We shipped it home, got it hung, and started learning more about Maurer and the art of his era in the early twentieth century. Then it just went on from there. We figured art was a better investment than a lot of other things because we'd have something we loved and enjoyed on our walls to look at. From then on, when I got a royalty check and we had some extra money, we'd buy a piece of art.

It has been a good investment, but it's also something that has enhanced our life. It's an interest that Lisa and I share; we're always reading up on artists and going to shows and museums. It's become an important part of our life.

We also love to travel, and when we do, we always go to galleries and museums. We've spent quite a lot of time in Provence in southern France, where I teach at the Mix with the Masters programs at Studios La Fabrique. Hervé Le Guil, the studio's owner, has taken me to places there that were the inspiration for van Gogh paintings. It's the most amazing thing to stand there and see a vista that van Gogh painted. It has been fascinating to learn about his life and the lives of so many other artists.

I've traveled a lot, both for my work and with Lisa, and I think it's important to learn about other cultures and to see how people in other countries live. Americans sometimes don't understand how much we have here, but they also sometimes don't understand what we are missing. In France and Italy and Spain, people seem to enjoy life in a way that we don't see here.

I think happiness really does come from the simpler things in life. When you are struggling to be better than the other guy, to work harder and get more, and you're working twelve to sixteen hours a day, I don't care how much you love what you do; that's tough. Now I think that waking up healthy every day, having a good meal, loving what I do, being happy with my spouse and family and having good friends are the things that make me happy. I also think it is important to be appreciative of everything you have in life, to enjoy it, and especially, to give back to others.

That's how I try to live now. Teaching and sharing what I've learned about recording is part of how I give back, and I hope this book is a help to people who are working, or want to work, in this profession.

APPENDIX A

Working with Al: What I've Learned

STEVE GENEWICK

*A respected engineer in his own right, with credits that include Bastille,
Michael Bublé, and Sam Smith, Steve Genewick has been assisting
Al in the studio for twenty years.*

I first met Al when I started working at Capitol Studios in 1994. Bill Smith
and I had worked together at Cherokee Studios, and after we both left there,
I was doing live sound and installations and Bill had gotten a staff job at
Capitol. One night, I ran into him and he told me there was a job opening at
Capitol. When he started telling me about how he was assisting for Al, I was
intrigued, because at that time I really didn't know who Al was. So, I went
by the studio the next day, and got the job. Bill was pretty much Al's main
assistant at that time. He really looked after Al, and ultimately, that's what I
learned to do as well.

I started out helping with general session setup, but Al's sessions were big,
and I ended up being the extra person who'd get pulled in to do whatever
was needed on his sessions. The first date I remember working on with him
was a Willie Nelson session with Jimmy Bowen producing. It was the biggest
setup I'd ever seen, a full orchestra with the conductor. Willie was singing
live in an iso booth, and I was the guy they'd send out to ask if he wanted
to come into the control room and listen to a playback. I'd go out, crack
the door, and Willie would be sitting there in the booth, which was filled
with smoke, with his headphones off. I'd ask, "Do you want to come in to
listen?" And he'd say, "No, I'll listen from here," and put his headphones

back on. Then I'd go back in the control room and say, "He's not coming in."

I guess I did okay because pretty soon it got to be that I was always the third guy on Al's session, after Al and Bill. I was also welcome to come in and hang out when I wasn't officially working on the session, and I did that all the time. I really wanted to learn. Then, since I was always around, it became natural that if Al ended up working in two rooms—say, mixing in one and overdubbing in another at the same time—Bill could be working in one room while I assisted Al in the other. That way, Al could bop back and forth and get double the work done. Sometime around 1998, Bill decided to go out on his own and I was the next guy in line. Al was having a superbusy period, so for about twelve years I did almost nothing but work with him.

Al was so booked, and so busy, it got to the point where we'd sit down and he'd tell me what was going to happen for the next six months. I was on staff, but I was basically getting my schedule from Al. I'd go to Paula Salvatore, Capitol's studio manager, and say, "This is what I'm doing the next six months, and you're about to get a call from Diana Krall's team for the month of June." Then the phone would ring, and Paula would say, "Oh. June. Yeah, I got you."

It rolled like that for long time, some big records, some little ones. It's not quite like that these days. The industry has changed and it's not as crazy busy as it was back then, but Al still works all the time and still knows his schedule pretty far in advance. Now, at Capitol, we also have Chandler Harrod, who knows the systems we use and has the right temperament to work with Al and his clients. Chandler's up to speed, and I'm able to also take on other projects, which works out great. But sometimes Al says, "I need you for this," and I'm there—I'd never leave him hanging. And there are some sessions where I just know I need to be there, like if Diana Krall comes in for a month, or Neil Young is doing live sessions with an orchestra.

How We Work

Al and I have been together so long that, no joke, sometimes we don't have to talk. In the control room, there's a lot of stuff that I will do, as Al's assistant, that I'll tell the other assistants not to do. "Don't do what I do. Don't reach over and grab that compressor. I might do that, but I've gained that trust with Al over twenty years." Because, in large part, I know what we're going to want to do.

Of course, if Al wants something specific, he'll tell me. As much as we do things the same way a lot, nothing's set in stone. There are days when he'll come in and say, "Let's use the 67 instead of the 47," or "I want to try this different preamp. I think it's going to work better for this song." Microphones are Al's main tool. After you've been engineering for a long time, you know what your tools do, and you have an instinct about what to use when. And Al definitely has more instinct than the rest of us.

When we did the Bob Dylan sessions, from the beginning we used the Sinatra U 48. Somehow, it's never a wrong choice. But on the second round of Dylan recordings, we had a different new mic that we liked, and Al said "Let's try it." We put it up, and Bob walked out to the mic and did his thing. But, after the first twenty minutes, I could see Al wasn't comfortable, so I said, "You don't like the mic, do you?" His response was, "No, let's change it." We had the 48 sitting there, warmed up and ready; I went out and took one mic off and put the other one on, and it was, "Yeah, that's the way it's supposed to sound."

Of course, we have a crew; I don't want to make it seem like it's just Al and I alone making a record. There are a lot of people involved and sometimes we'll just yell, "Swap out the vocal mic," or "Get a different pop filter," and someone will run and do it. But in this case, because Bob was standing in front of the mic, and he doesn't like to be around people he doesn't know, it was better for me to do it. The point being, Al wanted to see if something different might work better. He was willing to experiment, but he quickly realized that it wasn't quite right, and just as quickly we changed it back.

The Gear

Al has a lot of gear, and a huge collection of mics. He keeps everything in road cases that are in storage, except for a couple of items that live at Capitol, like the Evil Death Eye tube preamp, because we don't want them going in and out of the truck all the time and getting banged around. When we go to other studios, we'll often use his mics. But I'd say 50 to 60 percent of his mics don't come out of the road cases when he's at Capitol.

About ten years ago, Al had to get more cases because he was running out of space. We brought all his gear into the studio and I rearranged the racks, so they were labeled "Mix," "Record," or "Mix and Record." Now we can just call cartage and say, "On Friday, I need the mix gear," or "We're recording, so we need everything."

There's certain core equipment that hasn't changed in about fifteen years. For example, for recording, since all of Capitol's consoles have eight sends, Al has four reverbs that he monitors with, and I get the other four sends for headphone mixes. For recording, he always uses two sides of the Lexicon 480 with stock settings. Send one goes to a program called "Small + Stage," send two is "Medium + Stage," send three is either his Bricasti or the studio's EMT 250. Send four is always Capitol's chamber Four—that's his favorite.

All of the chambers at Capitol are technically very similar. If you ping them with a click, in length of time they measure within a millisecond or two of one another. They're all big, and the shapes are almost the same. But even though they look uniform, if you measure, they're all slightly different. They're sort of pie shaped, ten or twelve feet by eight feet, at the widest part maybe eight or nine feet wide. The narrow part is five or six feet. Number Four rings out at somewhere between 3.2 and 3.5 seconds. We don't use any predelay with it.

Al is very specific about how he uses his reverb. For mixing, we set up eight. Which ones we use have evolved over the years. Currently, we use the two settings on the Lexicon 480—feeding two mono aux sends into the 480 and two stereo returns out—the Bricasti, Capitol's chamber Four and a Lexicon PCM 96 drum plate program on which I've tweaked the parameters a bit. Send six is the PCM 96 "Large Warm Hall." Seven is a program called "Studio 40x40" in the TC Electronics Reverb 6000. And eight is a program called "Warm" in the 6000. That one's enormous, something like four and a half seconds. We call it the (trumpeter) "Chris Botti Reverb" because it was Chris who told us about it. It very rarely gets used, but we keep it set up. The rest range from 1.2 to 4 milliseconds. A lot of the reverbs Al uses are much smaller in size, and darker in color, than people would expect.

If he's got a reverb going that he likes, and someone asks him to make it longer, he'll throw a long one on top of it. He doesn't change what he has;

instead he'll add a longer one. That way he'll get the tail of the long one, but the actual ambient part of the sound will come from the first reverb and he'll still get the depth from the smaller one.

Very rarely does Al use just one reverb on a vocal. It's a combination. It used to be the EMT 250 and the live chamber, now it's the Bricasti and the chamber. For the shorter reverb in the combination, the predelay is set anywhere from 60 to 120 milliseconds, and it usually sits around 90 milliseconds. He just tweaks the mix of the two until, as he says, the little bell goes off in his head. That's literally what happens. He'll be dialing it in, doing this, doing that and playing with it. Then something happens, he'll stop, and never touch it again. After twenty years of watching Al, listening to what he does, and playing with the sounds myself, that's the best I can do to explain how he does it. We've never really talk about it. He probably can't even verbalize it, because so much of it is just feel for him. It's the same with the overall mix. It's literally about balance, and the magic for determining that balance is what's between his ears.

Historical Perspective

If you think about it, Al's been in the recording business pretty much since it started. As a child working for his uncle, whether he understood what was going on or not, he was hearing what was going on in the studio. Then, he went through the progression from recording in mono with one mic and the musicians, to four mics and the musicians, then it was eight tracks and the musicians and on from there.

When I started, we had forty-eight tracks, with all sorts of equipment to work with, and we put a microphone right on the snare drum. That's how I learned. And he was doing that, too, at that time. But he had the background of doing it differently. There's that story of how somebody told him one day to put a mic in front of the bass drum. That was a big deal. And, he just went on from there, adding mics on the toms and the hi-hat. The important thing is, he already knew what that drum kit sounded like before he put mics on the toms. When he had more tools available, he just used them to get a little more out of it.

So today, you might hear the toms really loud on recordings, and the only way to do that is to put individual microphones on them. Al does that, too, because he makes modern records. But for him, all along it has been about expanding on what he was already doing. Since he already knew what the instruments basically sound like, he could expand on that in the context of good taste. He wasn't learning something new by using new gear. He was just taking what he'd already done and adding another element into it.

When Al suddenly had a twenty-four-track tape machine to work with, he already knew how to make the record on eight tracks. With more tracks, he just had an expanded palette. He could add a couple more mics and he could make it bigger and stronger. He could double the vocal. He could do whatever he needed to do, but it was all based on his previous knowledge.

For students, I think it would be a good thing if they started more like Al did. Maybe they shouldn't be allowed to use a compressor or EQ for their first year. It would be: Learn how to record and balance, with a fader, a pan pot, and one reverb. Figure it out!

Mixing from Day One

If you watch Al during a big band session, you'll see he's constantly riding gain as he's recording. When the musicians come in for playback, he gets up and stands at the back of the room, and I stand over in the corner and hit play. We don't have to sit at the console and adjust things because Al's done his moves already while we were recording, and that's the rough mix.

You could actually say that we start mixing the day we find out about the gig. Before the session, he's thinking about who is going to be playing on the session, how he'll set them up, and what mics he'll use. Then, as soon as we start drawing the setup on a sheet of paper, Al's thinking about the mix and where he's going to pan things. Then he sets the band up in the room that way. If the guitar player and the acoustic guitar player are sitting to the left of the singer, he's probably going to pan them to the left.

For big bands, we do usually set them all up the same way. But there's almost always something new, like, "On the last record we did this with this person, did you like the mics we used, or do you want to go back to what we did on the record before that one?" Or "Do you want to try something new on the room mics, and maybe move them closer in this time?" Or "On this record they want it to be a little old-timey, so let's put the mics back a little bit and use ribbon mics for the room sound instead of the C12s."

The really fun dates are the ones where it's not a standard kind of session. Then the two of us will sit down and rack our brains a bit and collaborate. "What if we put these players here because we've got this person in the booth next to them?" and then Al might say, "Yeah, but these guys are going to bleed into this instrument. Do we care about that or not?" Or maybe, "We know all the musicians booked for the date, except there's an acoustic guitar player coming that's new. Maybe we should put him in a booth, because if he isn't that good, we might have to replace his part." Or "I talked to the producer and they want isolation on the accordion and the mandolin so they have to be in the booth."

Sometimes he'll have me draw up a plan, he'll also have something in mind and we'll put the two together. And sometimes it's, "We've got a four-piece band. I'm on a plane and I'll see you Tuesday." That's rare though. Al is very involved in everything he does. So, the instructions might be: "The usual big band set up, plus string overdub, fourteen, six, and four," and that's all he has to tell me. Then, I can send a text message to the setup person and he knows what mics to put up.

It's Not Really Magic

People listening at our sessions tend to say, "Wow, the band just starts playing and it sounds like a record!" They don't realize all that's gone on before everyone starts playing. If we're teaching, like at Mix with the Masters, the mixing workshops we do in France, I'll have a sit down with attendees beforehand and caution them that they have to pay attention the entire time—from the very beginning. Because a person might be changing drum heads or tuning the drums and just banging around, and Al may very well be in the control room setting a level on those drums. Or, if Al's out moving the sax mics and the drummer starts playing, I throw the mics up on the console and start getting the balance. When somebody's warming up on a horn, if you're watching, you'll see one of us lean over and set the mic preamp.

By the time we're ready to go with the whole band, we might have to check a few things: "Can we hear the trumpets? Something was weird." But often, it's just, "Yeah, we're cool. Just go ahead." They start playing and everybody says, "It's like magic!" But Al will say, "No, we've been working for the last thirty minutes; you just weren't paying attention to what we were doing."

On our sessions, you're never really going to hear an "Okay, now we're getting drum sounds. Can I hear the kick drum?" He might say, "Can you play for me?" But even that's rare. The magic generally happens very quietly. He'll ask the drummer to play, but he won't ask for just the kick or snare. Instead, while the drummer is playing, he'll push up the kick drum mic and listen to it, then the snare, then the overheads, then the toms. But that all happens in a matter of minutes. If it's a good player with a good-sounding kit, you're probably looking at three to five minutes to get drum sounds.

Since he's not going to EQ anything, and there's not going to be a compressor on the drums, it might just be, "Can we lower the overheads?" And somebody will run out and do it. Or, if he hears something weird, he might ask, "Can you hit the kick for me a couple of times?" and then, "Can we pull the mic back out a little?"

Sometimes, he'll ask them to play the style they're going to play for the session: brushes, if it's a ballad, or if it's swing with a big band, hitting hard. But eight out of ten times, we never even say, "Can you play for us?" They just start warming up and doing their thing and we just kind of do it when they do it so it comes together naturally.

An orchestra is a little different, because you have to get everybody situated in their seats. It's kind of like one big animal, with a lot going on at the same time. In that case, we'll be roughing in levels and then he'll say, "Can you run one down "on the stick?" Meaning, without the click, the prerecords or anything extra, just the conductor and the orchestra, so we hear them all together before we actually start recording.

If it's a really big orchestra, or a record with a rhythm section, big band, and strings together, we might say, "Can we just hear the rhythm section for a minute?" so he can balance them, I can get a headphone mix, and they can check their headphones. Then we'll have the rhythm section play with the horns, and then add the strings." Then it's, "Now can we hear the whole band play with the rhythm section?" for maybe half a song. Or "Play a section where it's loud." And then it's, "Okay, fine. We're done. Let's go."

All of that takes about five minutes, and it's a scramble. The first ten or fifteen minutes once the orchestra is seated can be a bit crazy. If there's other crew around, I'll say, "I'm going to headphones. You work with Al." And he'll be saying, "Violins down," or "Violas too loud!" One of the team has to be there to turn the viola preamp down so Al doesn't have to get up and walk across the room to do it while I'm trying to get the headphones worked out. There's usually another person in the control room, and a couple of people on the floor. We'll often have one person standing at the door, just waiting, in case someone says, "Viola 2 isn't working," and off they'll go to switch out the mic or fix whatever it might be with Viola 2.

But then we settle in, and once the orchestra plays it through one time, it's pretty much ready to go. The principals will come in to hear the playback: the conductor, the artist, producer, the concertmaster, and maybe the soloist, if there is one. Sometimes the rhythm section comes in, too.

Something important that I've learned from Al, and others, too, like Phil Ramone and Tommy LiPuma, is that no matter what we're doing, we try to get the principals into the control room to listen as soon as possible. We'll maybe do one take, and then it's "Headphones okay, everybody? Comfortable?" "Yeah, yeah. It's the first time we've seen the music." "All right, let's do it again. Play another one." And then Al will be the first one on the talk back, "Come in and listen."

When they come in, if we're doing something that's not exactly what they're looking for, they'll hear it right away and we can change it. But usually, you'll find that they hear the playback and then they kind of self-police. We often don't have to say anything at all.

Al might say to me, "The bass is too loud." Or "Does the snare sound funny to you?" Usually I'll agree, and he'll say, "All right, we'll see what happens." Then they come in for playback and everybody pretty much realizes what they need to change. When they go back out, you may see that the drummer's changing the snare drum. They generally just know. And if not, we can ask them, "Guitar's a little dull, do you think?" And the guitarist will say, "Yeah, okay. I'll brighten it up some."

It's the right way to do it: let them listen themselves and figure it out. And it's one of the things I love about working with Al. His sessions are very fluid that way. Connections have been made, everybody's friendly, and everybody feels involved.

What we're doing under the hood may be very technical, but it doesn't have to seem that way to the musicians. We're always laughing and having a good time and talking. I can't tell you how many times musicians will walk in and go, "It's you and Al today?" "Yeah." "Ah! Cool!"

And that's it. They're happy. The headphones are going to be good. The coffee's going to be good, and so is lunch. They're not worried about what's going to happen. Al's going to make them look good. And the musicians make us look great! I've seen and heard it so many times over the last twenty years, "Al pushed the faders up and it sounded great." It's a big part of how I learned. I know what sounds good because I've heard it sound good.

We're Making a Record Here. No, Really.
We're Making the Record Right Now!

Working and learning with Al, since he seemingly does so little, all I had to go on was to figure out what it was that he wasn't doing. I've watched him do automation on the console, and it's just lots and lots of tiny little moves. But over the years, it's become, "Ah, okay. I hear it now." I heard what he did, what he decided he didn't like, and how he went back and fixed it.

His EQ is really just his balancing. If he wants more low-end on the bass, he just pushes the track with the low-end mic up a little bit more. If he wants more attack on the bass, he just pushes the top-end mic track up. You want more rattle on the snare? Just push the bottom mic level up a bit.

How you learn from Al is that you listen, and you watch. He teaches by doing. When we're teaching together, we have a little bit of structure, but not a lot. Al will answer specific questions, like, "Why do you use AKG 414s on the toms?" But that usually will evolve into something interactive about how we get a drum sound. It's never specifics like: "Put the U 67 like this, and then set the compressor like this."

One of the most important things to realize is that, as soon as Al walks into the control room, we're making the record. I don't think about it. He doesn't think about it. We just do it. The second I walk in, I'm doing something, whether I'm prepping the Pro Tools or getting the console ready. If people watching don't pay attention, the first song will be done and they'll have missed the entire thing. If we're teaching, I warn them all and then I'll turn around and say to them: "Now!" And Al will be like, "What?" I'll tell him. "You're working. Just keep working." And I'll tell them, "See, when he does this, that's why you paid to be here. And you missed it!"

If Al was sitting at the console while that drummer was warming up, he got the drum sound. While the students are probably still waiting for the drum sound to happen, Al's on to: "Can I hear the bass?" The students are going to say, "What happened to the drums?" And he'll ask, "Was there something wrong with the drums?" "No, they sound great."

Al getting the guitar sound might have happened when he got up and walked out and talked to the guitar player. That may have been the guitar sound silver bullet the students were looking for, and they didn't even notice it!

There are times where someone says, "Can we get more presence on the guitar?" Ninety percent of the engineers who hear that will pop an EQ in and add 3K or whatever it is that brings it out. But Al might just make it louder. Literally, he might walk over and put the fader up a dB and it's, "Job done!" There's more presence on it because it's a little louder now.

For the mix, it might be that the guitar's too loud in the chorus, so he'll just drop it down in the chorus and then put it back up in the verse. He gets the presence he needs that way, rather than using compression to keep it even. It's just as easy for him to move the fader as it is to put a compressor on it, and moving the fader doesn't change the sound. He has control over the volume, but he still has a big, open sound on the instrument because it's not going through another set of electronics. Multiply that over fifty tracks, that's a lot of transformers and tubes, and it changes the overall sound.

It's the same thing with using fewer mics. Al might use half the microphones that other people use. I've seen him walk in on a string setup someone's done in the studio next door to where we're working, and he'll say to me, "Check this out. There are twelve mics on the strings. What the heck are they doing with all that?" Because we would have put four mics up for the same number of musicians. With so many more mics, they have to put the stands lower, so they're closer to the individual instruments they're supposed to capture. That's likely to lead to phase problems. All they really needed to do was to put four mics a little bit higher up and let the players play. The truth is, you're never going to be able to out mix the musicians; they're an orchestra!

It's not that Al doesn't ever use EQ or compressors. He owns a lot of both. He just doesn't use them until he needs to fix something. It's the same with plug-ins. He knows what they can do. If something is really messed up and needs to be fixed with a 3-band dynamic compressor or some whiz bang plug-in, or if a track is noisy and he knows I can de-noise it, he has no problem asking me to do that. And if a problem comes up when we're working that he knows a plug-in can fix, he'll be the first to say, "Don't worry. Steve can fix that later," so that he can keep the session going.

If it's something that's really out of whack, like a conga that's all over the place, he'll put a compressor on it to keep the dynamics in check. And these days he often uses Capitol's Fairchild on vocals both during the recording and the mixing. He's gone around a lot with different vocal compressors, which, of course, he uses mostly for the sound of the compressor itself, with maybe only two or three dB of compression. For a long time, it was always the Summit TLA 100, then for a while he used one of his own, the Al Schmitt/John Oram piece (Oram GMS [Grand Master Series] Al Schmitt Pro-Channel.) And once in a while, it could be a GML.

But about ten years ago, we put the mono Fairchild 660 on something and thought it worked great. And then for the next session it was, "Let's use the Fairchild again." It was just one of those things. We probably originally used it because we were trying to get out of a problem. Or maybe somebody asked for it, and it sounded great. I think Al went through the "I'd forgotten how good these things are" syndrome. Now the Fairchild is part of the current arsenal. He doesn't own one, so everybody knows that when Al is at Capitol, chamber Four, the Fairchild 660 and the NTI EQ are his. And if he's recording, he also gets one of the EMT 250s.

Sitting In
Al is really good about letting people sit in on his sessions so they can learn—

especially the new guys, who are always a little nervous about meeting him. As long as it's cool with clients and the producer, they're more than welcome to sit in the back of the room. Or they can come in when he's mixing. He really is an open book, and you can ask him anything you want—at the appropriate time. Don't ask him in the middle of a session. Ask him after, and in the meantime, watch what he does.

He invites them in, but if they overstep their bounds, one of us has to stop it, with "Don't do that again." Sometimes you can do that just with a look. Because, if people are going to come in and watch, they'd better be paying attention. They'd also better be ready to pitch in if needed. If someone in the studio says his headphones are broken, and I see a guy just sitting there, I'm going to say, "Why are you staring at me? The bass player said he had a problem—go fix it." If somebody says, "It would be great if we could get coffee," and you're just sitting there, you'd better be the one to go get it. Everybody's there to help, and someone who doesn't learn that quickly isn't going to work out on the job.

The Open-Door Policy

In general, we have the door open when we're mixing. There could be a nuclear holocaust, and if Al's mixing and in the zone, he doesn't care. He's focused and doesn't notice if people are in the room and talking. And, with the door open, often somebody recording in another room will pop in and say, "Al, what are you doing next week?" "We finish this on Tuesday." "Can you mix this on Wednesday?" "Yeah, sure." "Great."

Al couldn't be the kind of mixer who just works all day and never has a client show up. He'd hate it. He wants to see the musicians. That's really why we mix with the door open. He'll be mixing, and all of a sudden, you'll hear the orchestra next door go on a break. The doors fly open and the hallway gets full of people, and he'll stop the recorder. Because he knows, in two seconds, it's going to be. "Hey, Al!" and people are in the room. So, we take a break, we hang out, and then you'll hear from the hallway, "We're back." And everybody returns to their studio and we go back to work for an hour, till the next break when somebody else comes in. He loves it. It's what he lives for.

The Routine

Al is always on time. We tell new staffers, if he says, "I'll see you at ten a.m.," they'd better be ready for him to walk in at nine thirty a.m. These days, though, since he does Pilates in the morning and wants to avoid the worst of the traffic, he usually arrives at around ten thirty for an eleven o'clock start. And we get right to work. If we're mixing, we might have a cup of coffee and chat, "Did you see the game last night?" But then he sits down and he mixes. He'll stop for five minutes every hour or two to get an ear break. And at some point, we order lunch. When it gets there, we always stop, go to the lounge, and eat our lunch there.

You'll never see Al sitting at the console eating. You might see me sitting at the console eating, but that's rare, too. We stop to eat, even if it's just for ten minutes. Then we go back to work. We might pause in the afternoon again for five, ten minutes and have a coffee. Once in a while, if it's a nice day, we might go outside in the afternoon, and if it's just the two of us on a weekend, we might smoke a cigar. Then, usually by seven p.m., we're done and we go home.

In that eight hours, we get all the work done. When he comes in, he'll say, "I want to get three songs mixed today," and we'll do that within the confines of that schedule. Maybe we don't take the coffee break in the afternoon; we mix through instead. But our days are pretty much like that: Get going at a civil hour, have a nice lunch, go home at a decent time for dinner. But make sure you get all your work done in between!

Something else you need to know about Al is how deeply he cares, about both the music and the people. I don't know that I've ever heard him say, "Eh, it doesn't matter on this. It's good enough," or "Yeah, that'll do. We're done. It's fine." Whether it's Paul McCartney, or someone who's making their first album, whether he's getting paid a lot, or nothing, everybody gets the same treatment. That's his work ethic. The client might only have one day, so they only get one day's worth of work. He doesn't let anyone take advantage of him. But he treats everyone the same.

He's also never selfish with what he knows, or with giving someone a chance. He's always willing to share. And Al never is anything but above board when it comes to getting gigs. I think he figures if he gets the job, he gets the job. If he doesn't, he doesn't. There's always another job, so don't get precious about it. He'll never stab somebody in the back, he'll never put someone else down in order to get a gig. He might say to a producer, "Man, I always wanted to work with . . ." whoever it is. "If it ever comes up, I'd love to do that." But he'd never ask, "How do I get on that record?" That's not his style. He's got more class than that.

BILL SMITH

Grammy-nominated engineer Bill Smith has credits that include Toto, Queen Latifah, Whitney Houston, Natalie Cole, Chris Botti, John Fogerty, and YES. He worked with Al as both an assistant and an engineer for eleven years.

I'm from New York City originally and started my career at studios there, including Secret Sound, Quad Recording, and the Hit Factory. I moved to Los Angeles and had worked at Cherokee Studios for three years when I heard about an opening at Capitol Studios for a staff engineer position. I immediately went over to apply; I just showed up with a résumé and said I was there about the job. I interviewed with Michael Frondelli, who at the time was the recording director for studios. Michael was also an engineer originally from New York, and I think as soon as he recognized my familiar accent and confident manner, he felt that I'd be the right fit for the job.

Michael put me together with Al the second week I was at Capitol. I already had a lot of experience, and personality-wise, I think Michael knew that Al and I, being two New Yorkers, would work well together. Sometimes people don't understand the New York attitude and may take it the wrong way. But it's a straightforwardness you acquire when you're raised in the city. You don't waste time, you don't mince words, you pretty much just work hard and call it as you see it. I think these qualities, and a shared sense of humor, are a big part of the reason Al and I bonded as quickly as we did.

I worked at Capitol on staff exclusively with Al for four years, and when I decided to go freelance in 1996, he began to call me to work with him on sessions in other places that he went. For the next seven years, we worked in Los Angeles, Tokyo, New York, sometimes even back at Capitol, and I continued to learn everything I could from him.

Al doesn't really articulate what it is that he does, and I think in part that's because what you're doing as an engineer varies day to day. It's not something you can describe exactly. You may say, "Here's where I put the mic on the snare drum every single time, more or less," but everything else is up for grabs. Because the environment you're in, the musicians and the music are changing all the time and that alters your perspective and approach.

For example, on orchestral sessions, sometimes an arrangement may work on paper, or when the musicians are just playing it in the room by themselves. But when you try to put it on top of the track with everything else you've already recorded, it may be fighting four keyboards and three guitar parts. It doesn't come through the way it was imagined, and you may need to make certain things louder or softer. You can do that by grabbing the fader and changing the level in the control room, but it's better if you work with the conductor and producer to get it right at the source. And that's what Al's so good at; sometimes, he's actually engineering without touching a fader by helping to guide the dynamic in the room.

His process for making that happen is actually made up of two things that are diametrically opposed but working at the same time: what he's doing and what he's not doing. That's what many people don't see right way when they watch him work. He's hanging mics and he's pushing faders around and, yes, that's accomplishing a goal. But far more elusive is what he's not doing. And a big part of that is, he's not getting in the way. Sometimes, engineers or producers may be actively trying to accomplish something and to have some influence or control over the session. They want to put their stamp, or a specific kind of sound they're envisioning, on the recording. Al, on the other hand, is not really trying to exert control over anything in particular; he's just trying to capture a moment in time. He works around what's unfolding in front of him, moving according to where the musicians are heading and what they're doing. That's why he can go so easily from doing big band jazz one day to a trio the next day, to a rock and roll session with guitar amps and then to solo piano. He can move between all of those and still deliver the same high-quality product because he's injecting very little of himself into the situation.

If you ask him why he put a microphone in a particular spot, his answer will often be, "I put it where it needs to go." Knowing where to put it comes from his experience, but he also knows that there is no hard-and-fast answer to the question, because the best place to put it is where it works best on that particular day.

Some of what he does is very practical, like how he makes sure to place the mics so that they're out of the way of the musicians as much as possible. He understands that, as an engineer, the recording you're making doesn't matter as much as the ability of the musicians to do what they do. Sometimes people forget that the recording is secondary. They may think it's all about them: "I'm going to put the microphones where we're going to get the best sound." But if you think what you're doing is more important than what they're doing, you're wrong. Al always knows that what's happening out in the studio is far more important; his job is to translate it into the control room.

Al understands that his function in the room is to serve his clients to the best of his ability, so that when they walk out of the room at the end of the day, they're both satisfied and happy with what they've achieved. That's the only goal. It doesn't matter if he walks out of there completely satisfied. It's nice if he can get that, but it's not job number one.

Ultimately, Al's approach to how he records music is an extension of who he is as a human being. He's a highly intelligent, sophisticated, and classy person who has an elevated sense of style and taste. That extends from music to his appreciation of art, literature, fine dining, and fashion. You'll note that he's always well dressed—nice shoes, tie, looking good—and well mannered, and he brings that sophistication to his work.

Al is also very confident. As an engineer, people sometimes think they have to be tweaking knobs and turning dials all day to justify their paycheck. Al knows how to do all that, but he's intelligent and confident enough to know that he doesn't need the session to be about him twisting knobs. All he needs is for it to sound great when he turns the volume knob up for a playback. If he can achieve that in the simplest way possible, that's what he'll do. It's that same "stay out of the way" philosophy. Don't draw attention to yourself. Don't inject yourself where you don't have to.

That's not to say there aren't occasions when he has to step in to help move things along. Sometimes things can be going south, and, with all his experience, he may have a better solution than the ones that have been proposed. In that case, he may gently suggest an alternate approach. But again, when he does that, he's just trying to help out the artist and the producer. "I understand what you're trying to achieve here, but maybe we'll have better luck if we attempt it another way. What do you say we give this idea a try?" And nine times out of ten he's correct.

Because, when you're not inside the painting, it's much easier to see the painting as a whole. When you're a musician, and you're concentrating on the music and trying to play your part correctly, you're inside the painting. When you're the conductor, trying to make all the moves and lead the orchestra, you're inside. The artist is definitely inside the painting. Even the producer is focused on particular, specific things. But if you're an engineer like Al, you're listening to the whole thing. You're not inside at all. You're actually one of the few people in the room standing back and taking in the entire painting. That makes it much easier to see where things might be heading off track and you may be able to make a suggestion to rein it back in a little.

But Al will always do that that in a very respectful and considerate way. I've never seen him tell anybody that they're wrong—well actually, maybe I have, once or twice. But it's never presented as, "This is wrong; my idea is better." It's always, "I understand what you're trying to accomplish. Maybe this might be a better way to get there."

He'll never just oppose, or say no. No is bad; it denotes, "You don't know what you're doing and you're making a mistake." Al knows that there really aren't any mistakes, just alternate ways to do things. So, instead, he'll offer an alternative idea in a way that the artist knows is coming from genuine concern for him or her.

It's an awareness of what's going on psychologically with people that helps provide a comfort zone, like the detail of putting the mic far enough away from a musician so that he or she isn't worrying about it, and therefore unable to give his or her best performance.

For an engineer, sometimes even more important than the technical side of what we do is how we interact on a human level with the people we're working with. Al is a very supportive and genuine person and the artists and producers that work with him appreciate his enthusiasm and honesty, and that he genuinely cares about their work and their happiness. It's from Al that I learned that these qualities are what will give you a lifelong career.

Occasionally Al can get a little frustrated, but when that happens, it's still only because he's trying to do something that is in service to the artist. Sometimes that means saving them from themselves! A funny example of that occurred one time when we were mixing with Natalie Cole at Schnee Studio. I can't remember now which particular song it was, but Al had a great mix happening, and Natalie came in to listen. She said, "Guys, it sounds amazing! But how about adding a little more vocal?" And Al responded, "Okay, Bill, bring the vocal up a half dB."

A little while later she came back and listened again. "That's great, thank you! But I still think it needs just a little bit more vocal."

"All right. Let's add another half dB." She went out, we got that done, she came in again and once more it was, "I hate to say it, but just a hair more vocal." Al was by then getting the fishy-eyed look because he knew it was getting way too loud, but he asked me to do it anyway. But when she comes back in a final time and again suggested, "Could the vocal possibly be just a tiny bit louder?" Al walked over to the console, soloed the vocal, looked at her and asked, "How's that?"

She laughed and said, "Are you trying to tell me something?" His answer was, "I'm not trying." And that was that. Natalie said, "Okay, guys, put it where you think it sounds good and it's done."

Because she realized she was getting crazy with it, and that was his humorous way of telling her so. Of course, this was Natalie. He'd known her since she was a child so he could get away with it. Plus, Natalie was very intelligent, and not a shrinking violet in any way. He knew she could take it and would get the joke. So, you can see, he'll do what he needs to when an artist is heading somewhere he knows he or she will regret later.

That incident also speaks to his sense of self confidence, which I think originally came from growing up in the era that he did on the streets of Greenpoint, Brooklyn. His beginnings were not affluent, and it was hardscrabble. You had to learn street smarts: to stand up for yourself, to defend yourself and to be your own man. That meant you ended up self-reliant with the knowledge that you could handle whatever came your way. Living where he did at that time, there was a lot of Mob influence, wise-guy kind of stuff, and he could very easily have wound up working for the Mob instead of going into the music industry. I'm sure by the time he got dropped into that first session with Duke Ellington and the big band, a lot of his confidence and belief in himself were already established. He may have been as nervous as hell and doubting himself, but he still made it through. His confidence was already there, even if he didn't realize it until he got through that session.

Al has had a more profound effect on me than anybody else I've worked with. I admire him, and his friendship and guidance have meant a great deal to me. I've learned so much from him; not just in a work perspective, but a life perspective, too. One of the main things he taught me is that you have to keep moving forward, even in down moments. He's been very successful, but he's had tough times: the breakup of his marriages, getting sober. He's worked hard to get himself to a place in his life where he's content and happy. I can see in him now a sense of personal balance that wasn't always there, and it's great to know that he has reached that place in life.

NIKO BOLAS

Niko Bolas is a producer, engineer, consultant, and business developer who has recorded and/or mixed for artists from Warren Zevon and Los Lobos to Herbie Hancock, Sheryl Crow, Keith Richards, the Mavericks, Regina Spektor, Melissa Etheridge, and Neil Young, among many others.

Things about Al Schmitt: He is a master of both the art of recording and fearless adaptability. No matter the location, technology, or genre, he has a consistent drive to help make something great happen—now!

Personally, Al is a compass. If you are a little lost, or moving in an odd direction, he will let you know. For a minute, years ago, I tried to stop working on music, and to get a gig doing something completely different. Al said, "Don't be an idiot. They want you to be a mixer in residence here at Capitol—get it together. Besides, that way, I can come and hang out in your room!"

You hear a bit of Al on all of his records; there is something about them

Al and Niko: "Okay, if you'll do it, I'll do it."
(*Photograph by Chuck Olsen*)

that just feels good. There is no trick, no device, no technique, no magic room. Those components change all the time. What never changes is Schmitt's attitude, which (for any assistant who knows him) starts when you hear the rapid footsteps coming down the hall. Invariably, he is early and ready to go. Because of this, you can get first takes that are masters, and leave at night with emotional rough mixes that can never be beat.

Case in point: Neil Young had Al record and produce *On the Beach*. When they finished tracking, a few weeks went by. Al finally called and said, "Hey, Neil, when are we going to mix?" Neil answered with, "Al, it's already out! I mastered the roughs." When we recorded the *Storytone* record for Neil on the Sony soundstage, it was the same process; about half the finished record is the live balance done during the orchestra date. During those sessions on the soundstage, Neil was wearing this huge grin. Al looked over and said, "Shit, man. You know, I'm still waiting to mix *On the Beach*."

One December a few years ago, I walked into the office at Capitol and Al was sitting on the couch, reading *GQ* magazine. Of course, I immediately gave him crap about it. I said he should probably read *EQ* magazine instead, at which point he told me, "You know what? Ties and casual pants are in, and you really gotta dress better than wearing that T-shirt you live in." So, I told him, "Okay, if you do it, I'll do it; it's a bet."

I did not know at the time that Al is one of those fashion guys and owns a thousand ties. I soon found myself at Macy's buying a handful, and I've worn a tie to every session since. And so has he, going on several years now. I'll be damned if I'll be the first one to break. (It should be noted that weekends are now "casual.")

When Steve Jordan was producing Rod Stewart's *Soulbook* album, he had Al and me mixing each other's tracks in two rooms at Capitol across the hall from each other. I was mixing what Al had recorded, and vice versa. I tend to listen loud, and in the middle of the morning the phone rang. Our assistant Paul Smith answered, looked up, and said, "It's Al. He's got to talk to you." I grabbed the phone and Al yelled, "Hey! From *my* room, it sounds like you need more bass!" And, he was right.

Word to the wise: Never be late for an Al date. If you are on time, you are late. There is a very famous, researched and corroborated story about a certain engineer. He was assisting Al on a date back in the day at RCA, but he'd showed up late and had kind of left Al hanging. Al said nothing all day. But when the session ended, he walked him out to the loading dock, punched him, and said, "Never be late to my session again!" Enough said.

One time we were both recording Stan Getz at A&M for Herb Alpert. Al had started the record, and then Herb asked me to come in to do a couple of tracks. I brought my tube console and a bunch of gear in with me, and Al walked over and said, "Hey, are you really going to put that shiny horn Stan Getz is playing through this old piece of shit?" Then, when I began bringing the track up on the console, I started hitting the buss a little too hard. Al, pointing to the VU meters, said, "Hey asshole, it's *red* for a reason!"

A great Al memory of mine is working for him on the Sinatra record with Phil Ramone producing. The two of them never seemed to talk about the recording. They both already knew what it was they wanted to do, and they were doing it. That record got made with the latest new technology, with artists connected digitally all around the world, in the midst of a cascade of jokes, laughing, stories and insults.

One day Phil brought in some new binaural head-shaped microphones that he was experimenting with. I was playing with photography at the time, so Al and Phil and I set up the heads in a variety of compromising photos. How the music got done, I really do not remember. I guess that was the genius of Al and Phil.

Since Al's never really learned how to sugar coat conversationally, if you ask him for his opinion of what you're doing, be prepared for some simple Brooklyn responses. Like "This is terrible," or "I f@ckin' hate this." Of course, there is also the polite one-word "Really?" with that serious cutting stare waiting for your reply. The best feeling in the world for me is to get a "fantastic" or "absolutely" from Al.

While a mentor and an inspiration to many, I think Schmitt is still just an excited kid. One afternoon at Capitol, he was recording a big band for Pat Williams. He pulled me out of the hallway and said, "Get in there and listen to this." I stuck my head in, and he shoved me to the middle of the console and said, "No, I mean *listen* to this!" I had heard recordings many times in that room, in that spot, so I didn't know why he was so adamant until I realized the horn section was deeper and more brilliant than usual. I looked at him, and he had a huge Cheshire cat grin on his face. He said, "See? Follow me." Out to the studio we went, and he explained his latest. "I couldn't sleep last night thinking about the brass, so I moved them back two feet and raised them up on a riser another foot. Don't you love the difference?" This, from someone who has recorded nonstop for umpteen years. He still lies awake at night trying to figure out how to record better than yesterday.

In short: To me, Al is all about feel. He records and mixes straight from his heart. Instead of thinking, he trusts emotion and instinct. Making the player feel good is more important than which microphone will fit, the placement of instruments, or choices of treatment. The emotion you feel from the artist is (I believe) the only goal, and playing the recorded music back with that same emotion is Al's gig. That's the "Art of Recording."

Finally, I recommend that you never ride with Al when he is driving. I think it's something left over from a childhood in Brooklyn, or maybe his time in the navy (he is rumored to be a sharpshooter), but everything and everyone seems to be in his way. Take it from me, if you're going somewhere with Al, it's better if you drive.

JACKSON BROWNE

Singer/songwriter/musician and activist Jackson Browne worked with Al on his second and third albums: For Everyman *and* Late For The Sky.

When I met Al, I was looking for a mixer to finish my second album, *For Everyman*. I had been working with John Haney as engineer and coproducer, which worked fine, but when it came time to mix, we were having differences of opinion and I wound up bringing in Al in to mix the record.

Al was known to be a good mixer, but I didn't know until I met him that he'd worked with Sam Cooke, Ellington, The Jefferson Airplane, it's such a wild array. I don't think that everybody realized he had that kind of breadth . . . I think he had worked at RCA for a long time as maybe a staff producer . . . I mean Ann-Margret . . . The list is so long it's ridiculous. I really enjoyed his stories; they gave me a sense of the breadth of his career. Especially that wonderful story where, before he was even an experienced engineer, he was thrown into working with the Ellington Band. I think that kind of trial by fire must have forged in him a sense of adventurousness; and of always trying to find the best way forward. A sense of can do.

He's also wonderfully honest in the studio. One time, recording *Before The Deluge*, I was trying to get a bunch of people who were in the studio singing the chorus, to do a part that was just sort of humming along, like, "How about if here you just go, 'hmmmm.'" Al listened to about a minute of it and then walked out of the control room and into the studio, and he was just cracking up, saying, like he was the narrator, "And they came across the West, in covered wagons . . ."

He was a very diligent worker. When we worked on *Late For The Sky*, he didn't stay up late carousing with us. He had a son at home and tried to get

home as soon as he could. He came to work. He had a very strong work ethic, but, at the same time, he made everything so much fun.

When I wanted to remaster *Late For The Sky* for its fortieth anniversary, I didn't want to bother him with it since he'd already mixed it originally, and then mixed several songs again for a 7.1 surround compilation that I had done. So, I thought I'd just do it at the Mastering Lab with Doug Sax. It was originally mastered there with Mike Reece. Mike is no longer living, but I knew that they kept all the notes there. I went in to work with Doug off of Mike Reece's notes. And Doug of course, thought—and this is so human; everybody thinks that because so much has happened technically, we can improve this and make it sound better—Doug said, "I think we can make it a little more competitive."

But the thing is, Al and I had worked on that album at Elektra Studios, which was not his choice. He had never worked in there, and then when we mixed, wound up going to Hollywood Sound. But he wasn't in his favorite places to work, and he may have been miking things differently. He mastered to accommodate what we had done in the studio; that's the best way to put it. It was mixed and mastered by Al to make the most of what he had done for a singer who held notes too long, and who sang too loud—always. And if I did what Doug wanted to do in the remastering, to take away what Al and Mike had done would be to make it even more annoying than it was already. Anyway, I let Doug do what he wanted. I listened to it and then I booked time again a week later and came back and said, "Look, we just have to go back to what Mike did, because it's what he and Al did." And I hadn't wanted to bother Al with all this. I'm sure he'd be amused to hear about it all now, but I wasn't going to have him go to Ojai (where the Mastering Lab had relocated) with me and spend days laboring over something he'd already done once, and done perfectly. Especially since we had the notes. So, we not only used Mike's notes, but the Mastering Lab still had the exact same equipment, all the same gear!

Over the years I had fixed the vocal pitch on some songs that had always bothered me, on songs that were used in movies. But when I went in and wanted to include these fixed versions, Doug's engineer Robert Hadley, he just kind of raised an eyebrow, looked at me like I was completely crazy, and said, "What? You're going to put out the fortieth anniversary edition of the record—and you've fixed it?" That made me see the folly of my ways, and I said, "Well if we're not going to fix those things, let's not try to improve anything else. Let's put it out the way it went out originally."

Al taught me about drinking expensive wine. Of course, he wasn't drinking wine in the studio, and I can't remember how we got on the subject, but I remember saying, "Wait a minute. You'd drink a bottle of wine that cost a hundred dollars?" And he said, "Yeah. Well, you snort up what you've got in that little folded up piece paper and that costs one hundred twenty-five dollars, and that's gone in a night, too. Right?" And I said, "You enjoy it like that?" He says, "Yeah. Better than that." I never knew him to do any cocaine. I knew that he liked to drink wine, but when I remet him some years later, he'd stopped drinking.

But now he collects paintings. Which must be tremendously satisfying. In a way, he's got the nature of a collector, a sound collector, somebody who collects sounds and collects experiences. At its best, it's one of the most enjoyable things you can do, to hear music coming into being, to be there, in the best seat, and the first listener—the first person to hear the music. It's the best thing ever, and Al gets it to sound just right.

Really wild story. We went to go mix, a song from *For Everyman*, mixing at Heider's, the first album I did with him. We went in to mix and listen to the song and Al told the second engineer to go to the head of the reel and put some tones on it, while we went to get coffee. We came back and started listening and we get to the solo and suddenly it's just *beeeeeeeeeeeeep*! The second engineer had recorded the tones across all twenty-four tracks, in the middle of the song at the solo. Evidently, there were some grease pencil marks put there during the making of the record to let us know when the solo was coming up and he put the tones there without listening.

When we got over the shock, he said, "Well, Wally Heider will have to give us some time and some money to recut it." But then he looked around, and the second engineer wasn't there. I guess he saw what he'd done and he split. Al went to the other guys working there and explained what happened and said, "You'd better go to his house, and make sure he's okay. Just go find him and tell him I said it was just a mistake. And that's the last time he'll make *that* mistake." But he just treated it like it was a mistake. He was so great; he was so caring in the way he let this guy know that it wasn't the end of his career.

We were on our way to the studio one day and we stopped at the bank and there was a girl there who was just so fine. And he was unbelievable. I don't know how to say it . . . he was just so . . . he started chatting her up right away, right there in the teller line, and he was so on point. I never really knew how to talk to girls, and I thought, *Wow, this is how it's done.* And I think she appreciated him. He wasn't off-putting at all—he was very smooth. I don't know if *smooth* is the word. Just potent. I don't know what to call it.

He has an elegance, and a style. That jazz look that you see in that Jim Marshall book about the Monterey Jazz Festival. Sartorial elegance. Al comes from that world. That's the other reason the psychedelic connection seems so incongruous.

We did make that record [*Late For The Sky*] in the shortest amount of time I have ever spent making a record. My first record took four months, and for everyone I knew that was unheard of.

Like, why would you spend so much time in the studio? As a matter of fact, the reason we recorded at Elektra was that David Geffen, who was newly the head of Elektra Records, wanted somebody to record in his studio, wanted me to record in his studio, so people would think it was a good studio and work there. It was a good studio. Jac Holzman had built it. But it wasn't as good as other studios for the simple reason that the studio staff had an outsize sense of their job security, and they didn't really try as hard, and it wasn't completely dialed in. Fritz Richmond, who seconded for Al, had been a musician in the Jim Kweskin Jug Band and was a really good friend of mine—I was happy, really happy, that he was there and he made a great difference in that record. He had worked a lot with Paul Rothchild. But Al didn't really need an engineer; he just needed somebody to run the room. I'm not sure that it was . . . I don't think it was a great place for Al to record. I don't think he was sure what he was hearing, I don't think the monitors were quite dialed in and we ended up working in that room solely because Geffen asked me to. He said he'd give me a really big break, a discount on the cost of the studio time, and then later completely forgot about that, and still doesn't remember that he said it.

We worked there for that reason. But I was going to work with Al because it was really fun working with him finishing the *For Everyman* album and thought it came out really good. It wasn't to bring the record in on time. We cut that record in three weeks. For a jazz record, that's taking your time. But for a rock record and the way I worked, I'd spent more than four months on my first album, and my second album took probably six or seven months. I was in there still writing songs . . . .

But with Al, it was different. We worked beautifully and quickly, and the reason we didn't actually finish in four weeks was that I got a cold, so we took off about a week before I finished up vocals. So, five weeks from start to finish. And I can hear it on some of those vocals—my head was stuffed up on some songs. But I was really happy to work quickly, and I likened it to the impressionist or the plein air painters who go out and make a painting in a day. Why not? It was also the first album where I had the same band on every song, *Late For The Sky*. Same bass player, same drummer, and David Lindley—I wanted to get that feeling that you have with a band on the road. It was David Lindley playing violin, or slide or electric guitar, it was Jai Winding playing organ, when I played piano, and piano when I played guitar. With Lindley, it's always been more like being in a band together. Yeah, it was the first time I had settled into getting to do a bunch of songs with the same people every day and work out the best arrangements that way, and for that, Al was just perfect.

What I have noticed throughout my career, is the best shows were the ones I didn't see coming. If you were nervous about being in the studio that could be a factor, too, so having that manner that Al has, of putting everybody at ease, and enjoying yourself and enjoying the sound of everything as its going down—it is so important. It goes into the music.

The music is saying so much more than you could ever say with words. There is still a lot of little kid in Al. There's a great lyric by Taylor Goldsmith of Dawes, with a long list of things he gets to do because he's still a little kid, ending with I'm playing in a rock band! Because I'm still a kid!

It is about finding your inner child, and finding what Ed Cherney calls the mind of the beginner. Somebody who is always discovering something new.

Al is a connoisseur of players, of musicians. He knows everybody for how they play and how they sound and how they *can* sound, because he enjoys it on that level, and seeks that in a session—to put it together in the best possible way.

DIANA KRALL

Multiple Grammy and Juno Award–winning jazz pianist and singer
Diana Krall has made twelve of her albums with Al as engineer.

What Al has is more than knowledge. I've sat next to him many times while he's mixing, because there is such a vibe. It's as if you're sitting next to a great jazz pianist like Hank Jones—who played with Ella Fitzgerald and Charlie Parker—someone who has all the knowledge but also all the brilliance and intensity.

Sitting next to Al, watching his hands move on the mixing board, and seeing the amount of focus, concentration, and artistry that he has, is an amazing experience. He goes into his own zone where he knows what to do and he makes his moves. There's a gentle, quiet beauty to it, almost like you're watching a dancer.

He and Tommy LiPuma and I had so much fun making records together. There's a really beautiful photo I took of them talking in the studio that's on the back of my *Turn Up the Quiet* album cover. I always laugh about that picture and say, "Tommy's probably describing the roast rabbit he had last night for dinner." Because they could be talking about food, or something very deep within the music, about art, or a specific painting. Or it could have been a story about Jefferson Airplane. I'd always ask them to tell me stories about their wild days when they traveled together. They had a great partnership, like the partnership of Ray Brown and Oscar Peterson, great musicians who knew each other so well. Al and Tommy enjoyed everything that they did together.

Tommy always sat out in the studio, and if I was doing a take, Tommy would say, "One more," or "That was great," but then we'd always defer to Al. We'd say, "Hey, Al," he'd go, "Yeah," and I could tell, *He's going to want another one.* "Where are we at, Al?" "You might want to come in here and see what's going on." So, we'd go in, listen, and do another take. Then it was, "Hey Al," again, and hopefully his response was, "That was a really good one." Because that was all he had to say.

You have to learn your craft; that's how you get the tools to express yourself. But Al is an artist as well. He's been around, and behind the glass, a long time. He's seen everything, and he knows how artists work. He will help you realize what you want and what you're trying to hear. Even if you say you want more purple on something, he'll understand what you're talking about.

Once in an interview he was asked the question, "How do you make Diana Krall sound like that?' He answered, "I put the put the microphone in front of her." When I read that I thought, *Well, not exactly!* He's very, very humble. There's no ego going on at all.

Something else I love about Al is that he's very affectionate, even with people you'd think might bristle, who are not demonstrative and you'd think, *That's not their style.* Al won't have it. He'll just say, "Aw, give me a hug!" He's one of the warmest, most positive, emotionally direct and fair persons I've ever met in my life.

Al knows how to communicate with artists. He'll do things like reference old movies. "Have you seen that movie *Picnic*? It reminds me of this." And working with him, there's an incredible trust. You know that if something isn't right, like the tuning, or something technical, he'll stop and say, "Nope; one more." You trust him completely, like you would any great artist. He knows more than you do; he hears more than you do.

Another thing about Al is, when things get tough, he's going to speak up, and he'll have your back, all the time. He'll be there for you and understand if you need to jump in the car and drive around the block a few times. I always go to him when there's a problem. I'll take him aside and say, "Can I talk to you?" and he'll be very, very honest. I've confided in him greatly about some of my deepest fears surrounding this crazy life we lead, and he's counseled and reassured me numerous times

Working with Tommy and me, Al would often be in the middle. He would never take sides; he would just listen. I'm sure I went to him as much as Tommy did, me saying, "He's driving me nuts," Tommy saying, "She's driving me nuts." Al will say, "This is how you make a record. You do it by hammering things out. Sometimes that means you have the argument that needs to be had, and we'll figure it out from there. That's what we do." He just always knew how to handle the situation, and then at the end of the day, we'd laugh at it over dinner.

One of the last times the three of us went to dinner together, I just sat there and listened to them talk, about everyone from Randy Newman to Barbra Streisand, Dan Hicks, and Bob Dylan.

Al and I have wonderful conversations about Doris Day. Or just life. Sometimes, he'll send me a text just saying "I love you," and how great is that? He always comes to my concerts, and he's always been a cheerleader for me.

There's so much more, like the compassion he and Lisa have for rescue animals. So many times, I've called him and found out he was at the animal hospital with one of their dogs. And their passion for art, for cooking, for kids . . . . He recently told me about the sessions he did with students at Avatar Studios in New York. He was so excited about what the kids were doing. His enthusiasm, his excitement and openness about young people is inspiring. I've worked with Al for twenty-five years; I've done almost all of my records with him. But as much as he's done, Al is ageless; I think he's only ever going to be just age thirty-five!

GEORGE BENSON

Over the past four decades, jazz icon George Benson has recorded a dozen albums with Al, from 1976's landmark Breezin' *to 2013's* Inspiration: A Tribute to Nat King Cole.

In 1975, I signed a contract with Warner Bros., and we set up a record date. When I got to Capitol Studios for the session, there was nothing to do, because Al had already set up long before we got there. Everything was in place; the only thing he needed was my amplifier, and for me to plug in my guitar. The rest of the band were all miked up, too. And then, I met Al. He was just an ordinary fellow, and we had some brief conversations, but he was very quiet. The album we were going to work on was *Breezin'*, of course, which later went to the moon.

The first thing I really noticed—and this was very important—was that the first take of the first song we recorded came out perfect. Matter of fact, we used it on the album. That is what Al is so good at. And also, the sound of my guitar was the best I had ever heard.

Bobby Womack, the writer of the song "Breezin'," happened to walk in while "This Masquerade" was playing back and he said, "Who in here has a voice like that?" Al said, "George Benson." "But George Benson is just a guitar player!" "Yeah, but he's also a singer." We knew we had recorded something special, but it was Al who also made it sound special.

Al changed the course of my whole career because my sound became much more acceptable. He did the same thing for the guitar that he did for my voice. He found the right sound that I thought I should have. That's what he does, and that's where he excels.

I'll tell you another story of how he saved me one time. The only live album we'd ever done for Warner's, *Weekend in L.A*, had the song "On Broadway" on it. We called it *Weekend in L.A.* because Friday, Saturday, and Sunday, we had two shows a night, and from those nights, we thought we

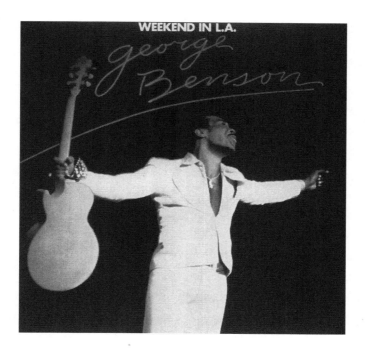

could get enough material to get a fairly good-sounding live album. So, on Friday night, the first night, we had a truck in the back, the Wally Heider truck. It was the first time I saw Al working in a mobile unit.

During the second show, we did "On Broadway" for the second time. The first time, to me, was a disaster, because it wasn't the right tempo and I didn't get the right performance. The second performance was magnificent. I said, "Al, can I have a copy of that tape?" He made me a cassette copy, and we played it on the boom box at the hotel, on the pool patio, all night long. People wouldn't let me turn it off.

Afterwards, we got ready to listen to the all of the recordings and to condense things down to a 2-track. We went to Tommy LiPuma's house and we were listening back, but the only thing I really wanted to hear was "On Broadway." I knew there was something to that record that was going to attack people; they were going to have to pay attention to it.

Tommy played the first version of "On Broadway," from the first show on Friday night. I said, "Hold it, Tommy; what version is this?" He said, "The first show on Friday night." I said, "Take that off, man; play the second show from Friday night." They started looking for it and he said, "George, I cannot find that tape. I think that we ended up recording over that tape." I said, "What do you mean?" He said, "We recorded so many songs, and we had to use so much tape, we started running out of tape. So, I just grabbed one of the old reels; I figured it was no good because it was one of the early sessions."

Man, when I heard that, I was broken. I got out of the chair, and I started walking back to the hotel, which was a couple of miles away. But when I got to the hotel, Tommy gave me a call and said, "George, come on back out, I think I found it." I took a car back, and when I got there he said, "Now I'm going to put on the hit," and he stared playing it.

He said, "That's better!" I said, "Tommy, that is a hit record if I ever heard one." Thanks to Al's not ever wanting to erase anything, he had put the tape somewhere special, so it was safe. Nobody knew where it was but him, probably; I'm only guessing at that. But he saved my career. "On Broadway" is one of the most important songs I've ever recorded, that live version which he captured so eloquently, and he captured every bit of it. The fact that he did that made me look at him very differently and made me very glad to have him as part of our team.

SHELBY LYNNE

Shelby Lynne is a Grammy-winning artist whose work spans country, rock, pop, and soul. Her first collaboration with Al was her tenth album, Just a Little Lovin', *a tribute to the great British soul singer Dusty Springfield.*

Let me tell you how I met Al. It was 2008. I was signed to Capitol Records at the time, and I wanted to record Dusty Springfield songs, so I called Phil Ramone, who was a friend of mine. I said, "This is what I want: I want Capitol Records Studio A. I want to cut to 2-inch tape, and I want Al Schmitt." He said, "Okay, darling, I'll make a call and get back to you." Ten minutes later he called me back and we were on.

At the time, nobody was using tape. Hardly anybody uses tape now, either, but I'm a tape girl. I love it, and I knew Al understood it. Now, I could tell he wasn't thrilled about the idea, but he did it for me, and it was one of my best records, so that was that!

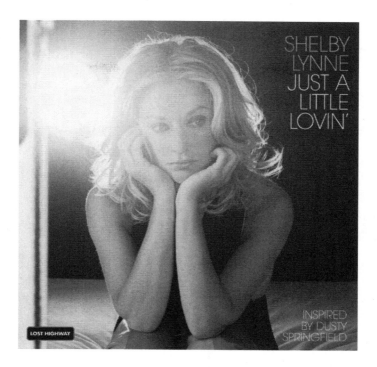

Al really knows how to record vocalists. It's basically a jazz approach, and it's what I wanted on that record. It was the perfect pair to have Al and Phil. They'd done so many cool projects together. Phil was a friend, but the first day of the sessions for *Just a Little Lovin'* was the first day I met Al. And we were off and running, in the first hour.

Al is a perfect gentleman, and he's completely in control of everything in the studio. Everything was wired and ready to go, of course, when I got there. We hit it off instantly. I said, "You know, I have a 2-track tape machine in my bedroom," and after that, we had a running joke about my thing for tape machines; he kind of picked on me about it.

We did the record in five days at Capitol, and it was an incredible experience. Since then, I've worked with Al on mixes, he's helped me with ideas, and he's shared his expertise in knowing how to record.

In the studio, he just puts the mic up there, gets it sounding good, and lets the artist be. That's when artists shine, when they get to be comfortable in a setting where they can not only hear themselves, but they can hear the room. That's a big part of his expertise; he knows how to record a room, and a vocalist—plus everything else.

Everything was pristine on that record, and we kept it small, a five-piece and vocals. A lot of those tracks are just two takes. Al's always ready, and I think that's also what a singer wants, to be ready. I like to just sit down and cut, with no waiting and no dinkin' around. Al is ready to go way before anyone else. He's in control, and it's incredible to watch.

I also admire his guts. There are engineers and there are superengineers, and Al goes beyond that. He's the best that's ever been. He has taught me how to understand the possibilities of a room. And when Al mixes, he mixes a record as it's being recorded. That's something that is not really understood now because everything is so post oriented. I'm pretty much cut from the old school. I might have been better off fifty years ago, but I do enjoy the recording process, and Al and I understand each other. With technology, anybody can make a record. Al knows how to do it that old-school way, and he makes it feel a little ancient, which for me, is my personal preference. He appreciates a real singer and real musicians, and that first or second take that should be the record. It's a master product when it goes down to the board.

We've become friends and we always feel like family. It's been a joy to have known Al and get to stand beside him and make a record. That way of recording is kind of going away in our time. But to be able to make one of my finest records, with some of my finest moments as an artist, with Al, was one of the greatest joys of my life. I still get compliments all the time on that record, and the way it was recorded. It's just a privilege to have worked with him.

APPENDIX B

Recording Session Layout Diagrams

These session diagrams show the layouts, mic choices, and mic placements for some of Al's important albums and artists.

NEIL YOUNG'S *STORYTONE* SESSIONS

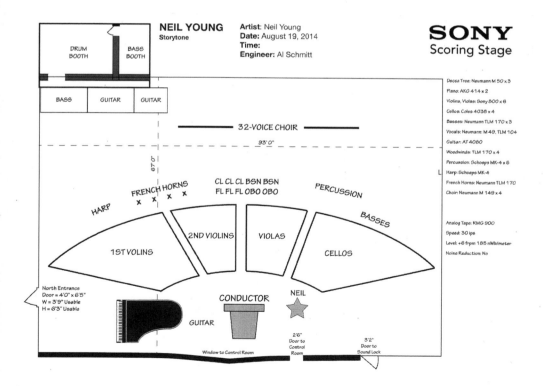

(Illustration adapted by Bill Gibson)

RAY CHARLES AND BETTY CARTER'S
THE RAY CHARLES AND BETTY CARTER SESSIONS

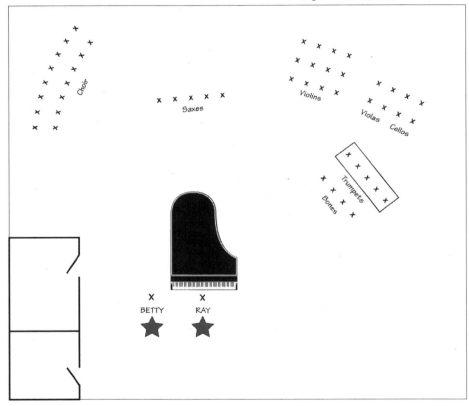

(Illustration adapted by Bill Gibson)

PATRICK WILLIAMS'S *AURORA* SESSIONS

PAT WILLIAMS BIG BAND
Aurora

Artist: Pat Williams Big Band
Date: 3-26-15
Time: 10 a.m.
Engineer: Al Schmitt/Steve Genewick

Bass: Neumann M 149 x 2

Kick: AKG D12
Snare: AKG C 452 20-dB Pad
              Shure SM57
Hat: AKG C 452
Toms: AKG C414 x 3 20-dB Pad
Overhead: AT5045 x 2

Piano: Neumann M 149 x 2

Guitar: Royer R-122v
              AKG C 460

Brass Section: AT4080 x 2
Sax Section: AKG C12 VR x 2v

Saxes: Neumann U 67 x 5
Bones: Royer R-122v x 5
Trpts: Neumann U 67 x 4
              PAD omni

Vocal: Neumann U 47

Perc.:   AKG C 414 x 2
              Neumann SKM 140 x 2
Tympani: Neumann U 47 fet

(Illustration adapted by Bill Gibson)

FRANK SINATRA'S *DUETS* SESSIONS

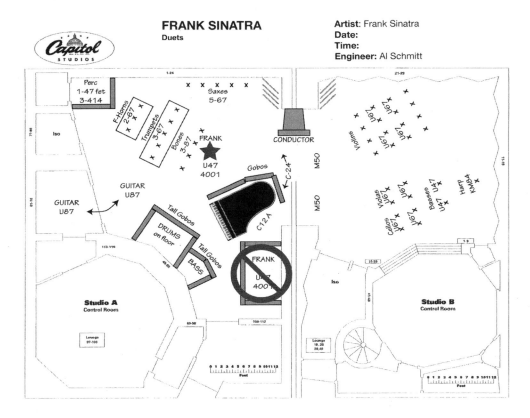

(Illustration adapted by Bill Gibson)

BOB DYLAN'S *FALLEN ANGELS, SHADOWS IN THE NIGHT,* AND *TRIPLICATE* SESSIONS

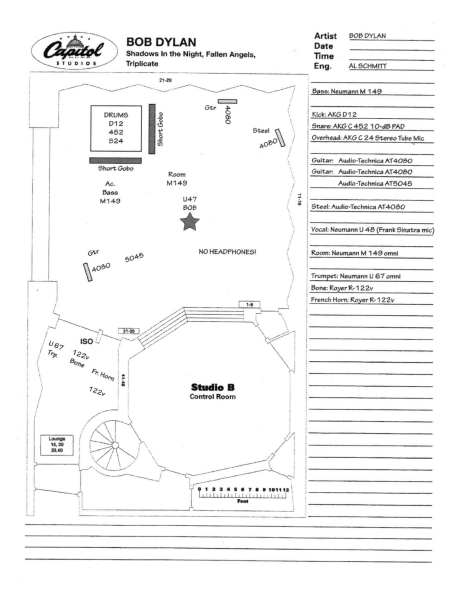

(Illustration adapted by Bill Gibson)

DIANA KRALL'S *TURN UP THE QUIET* SESSIONS

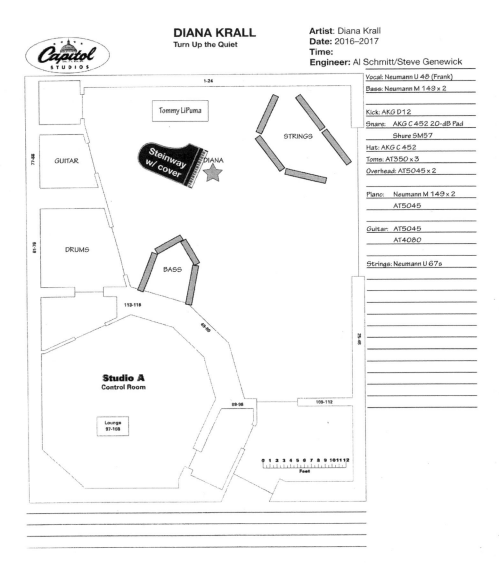

(Illustration adapted by Bill Gibson

TOTO'S *TOTO IV* SESSIONS

TOTO
TOTO IV

Artist: TOTO
Date: 6-1-81
Time:
Engineer: Al Schmitt

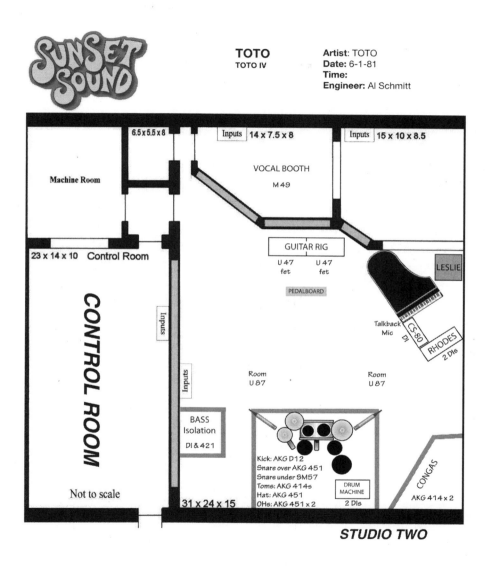

(Illustration adapted by Bill Gibson)

APPENDIX C

Selected Discography: The Essentials

Bob Dylan, *Shadows In The Night*, 2015

Paul McCartney, *Kisses on the Bottom*, 2012

Shelby Lynne, *Just a Little Lovin'*, 2008

Diana Krall, *Quiet Nights*, 2009

Ray Charles, *Genius Loves Company*, 2004

Diana Krall, *Look of Love*, 2001

Frank Sinatra, *Duets*, 1993

Shirley Horn, *Here's to Life*, 1992

Natalie Cole, *Unforgettable*, 1991

Claus Ogerman, *CityScape*, 1982

Toto, *Toto IV*, 1982

Steely Dan, *Aja*, 1977

Al Jarreau, *Look to the Rainbow*, 1977

Joao Gilberto, *Amoroso*, 1976

George Benson, *Breezin'*, 1976

Claus Ogerman, *Gate of Dreams*, 1976

Barbra Streisand, *The Way We Were*, 1974

Jackson Browne, *Late For The Sky*, 1974

Dave Mason, *Alone Together*, 1970

Jefferson Airplane, *Volunteers*, 1969

Jefferson Airplane, *After Bathing at Baxter's*, 1967

Sam Cooke, *Sam Cooke Live at the Copa*, 1964

Henry Mancini, *Hatari!*, 1962

Sam Cooke, Another Saturday Night (single), 1962

Ray Charles and Betty Carter, *Ray Charles and Betty Carter*, 1961

Henry Mancini, *Breakfast at Tiffany's*, (soundtrack) 1961

Sam Cooke, Bring it on Home (single), 1961

Sam Cooke, Cupid (single), 1960

Henry Mancini, *The Music from Peter Gunn*, 1959

Gerry Mulligan and Chet Baker, *Reunion*, 1957

NOTES

Chapter 2

1. Born Lester William Polsfuss, Les Paul was a guitarist, songwriter, recording artist, and inventor. He began his career in country music in the 1950s, performing as a duo with his first wife as Les Paul and Mary Ford, selling millions of records and hosting their own television show. Paul went on to further fame in jazz and popular music and as an inventor. Credited with building the first solid body electric guitar, he was also one of the first to experiment with multitrack recording and signal processing, such as reverb and tape delay. Paul is the only person to be included in both the Rock and Roll Hall of Fame and the National Inventors Hall of Fame.

2. A percussive style of playing blues on piano, the musical genre boogie-woogie is characterized by a bass rhythm of eighth notes in quadruple time and a simple, often improvised melody. Believed to have originated in the 1870s in African American communities, it became popular in the 1920s and was often incorporated into the music of the swing bands of the 1940s.

3. Swing music is a form of jazz usually played by large dance bands, with a strong rhythm section, a basic melody with simple harmonies, and improvised solos. Danceable swing by big bands and their leaders, including Benny Goodman, Duke Ellington, Woody Herman, Glenn Miller,

and Artie Shaw was the dominant form of American popular music from 1935 to 1946. Swing later blended with other genres to create new styles, from country and western swing to the urban-style new jack swing of the 1980s and early nineties and the swing revival of the 2000s played by bands like Big Bad Voodoo Daddy and the Brian Setzer Orchestra.

4. Most popular in the early 1940s, the jitterbug is an acrobatic jazz variation of the two-step dance for couples, consisting of a few standardized steps augmented by twirls, splits, and more, performed chiefly to boogie-woogie and swing. The Lindy Hop, probably named for aviator Charles Lindbergh, is a variation of jitterbug that originated in Harlem, New York City.

5. Jimmie Lunceford was a jazz alto saxophonist and the leader of a swing band that rivaled the orchestras of Duke Ellington, Benny Goodman, and Count Basie. His band differed from other big bands of the 1930s and 1940s in that it was known more for its ensemble playing than for its soloists, and for the fact that, while most bands of that era used a four-beat rhythm, the Lunceford orchestra developed a distinctive two-beat swing, creating a sound known as the Lunceford 2-beat.

Chapter 3

1. Thomas Dowd (1925–2002), born in New York City, was a recording engineer and producer starting in the 1940s. He also worked in nuclear physics, including on the Manhattan Project, where, during World War II, the atomic bomb was developed. Dowd went on to become chief engineer and a staff producer for Atlantic Records, where he helped popularize 8-track recording and the use of stereo. He recorded hits for artists that include the Allman Brothers Band, Booker T and the MGs, Eric Clapton, Bobby Darin, Ray Charles, John Coltrane, the Drifters, Aretha Franklin, Lynyrd Skynyrd, Thelonius Monk, Charlie Parker, and many more. A Technical Grammy Award recipient, Dowd is a Rock and Roll Hall of Fame inductee and the subject of the Grammy Award–nominated documentary *Tom Dowd & the Language of Music*.

2. Ribbon microphones, also called velocity microphones, use a thin, electrically conductive metal ribbon suspended between the poles of a magnet to sense sound waves. Typically ribbon mics are bidirectional: they pick up sounds equally well from both sides of the microphone. Early ribbon mics were both delicate and expensive and in general not to be used on loud instruments, but many of those made with today's materials are much more robust.

3. Jazz drummer Norman "Tiny" Kahn was known for bringing the improvisational feeling of small band drumming to his work with big bands, playing fills and lead-ins that helped propel the band. A musical but straightforward player, he was credited with understanding when to leave space and never playing too loud.

4. Ahmet Ertegun (1923–2006) was a songwriter and businessman born in Istanbul, Turkey, who in 1947 became cofounder and president of Atlantic Records. Ertegun was known for discovering, championing and/or signing, rhythm and blues, rock, and soul artists, including Ray Charles, the Drifters, the Clovers, Aretha Franklin, Cream, Buffalo Springfield, the Bee Gees, Bette Midler, Wilson Pickett, and the Rolling Stones. He also wrote blues and pop songs that became classics, such as "Chains of Love" and "Mess Around."

5. Dynamic microphones consist of a wrapped coil of fine wire attached to a delicate diaphragm and suspended in a magnetic field. When sound waves hit the diaphragm, the coil moves and an electrical current is generated that replicates the energy of the sound wave. Condenser mics employ a capacitor comprising two plates with a voltage between them; one of the plates is made of very light material and acts as the diaphragm, which vibrates when hit by sound waves. Condenser mics generally produce low levels that need to be amplified. Tube microphones are condenser microphones that use tubes to amplify their signal.

6. Gerald Joseph Mulligan (1927–1996) was a composer, arranger, saxo-

phonist, and bandleader known particularly for his unique, light style on baritone saxophone. An innovator in the post-bebop genre known as cool jazz, Mulligan played with, and arranged for, the highly influential Miles Davis Nonet whose recordings were compiled into the 1957 album *Birth of the Cool*.

Chapter 4

1. Some sources say that East Coast jazz had a harder edge, that West Coast jazz was smoother and more lyrical, and that it encompassed film scores and television music and was thus not as pure a form of the genre as East Coast. But while magazines discussed the perceived differences, jazz fans and the musicians themselves seem to have been indifferent to the labeling.

2. *Peter Gunn* was an American TV series that ran from 1958 through 1961.

3. Owsley Stanley (1935–2011), born Augustus Owsley Stanley III, was an audio engineer and chemist who became a San Francisco Bay Area legend during the hippie era in the 1960s. Under his nickname, "Bear," he was the soundman for the Grateful Dead, often making live recordings of their shows directly from the audio mixing board. Famous as an evangelist for the use of psychedelic drugs, Stanley is believed to be the first private individual to have manufactured large quantities of LSD.

Chapter 5

1. Compression (or limiting, a more radical form of compression with a ratio of 20:1 or above) is a form of controlling the dynamics of a piece of recorded music with audio signal processing that lowers the volume of the loud sections of the recording and raises the volume of quieter sections. It is often used to make the overall volume of a song seem louder so that the song will stand out in comparison to songs played before and after it, thus creating what are sometimes called the "loudness wars."

2. The three main microphone pickup patterns are: omnidirectional, also called nondirectional, which, in general, picks up sound from all directions in a 360-degree pattern, although the actual pickup pattern will vary with the size, shape, and design of each microphone; cardioid, a heart-shape pattern that rejects sound coming from the microphone's rear; and bidirectional or figure-8, which picks up sound from the microphone's front and back and rejects sound at its sides.

3. The Decca Tree is a technique for making stereo recordings that was developed at Decca Records, which was originally a British company founded in 1929. The actual microphone stand, the "Tree," was designed by Decca engineer Roy Wallace in the early 1950s. Three omnidirectional microphones, traditionally Neumann tube condenser M 50s, are placed in a triangle approximately eight to twelve feet above the floor—depending on the size of the room and orchestra—just behind the conductor with the left and right mics about six and a half feet apart, and the center mic a little less than five feet in front of the others. The left and right mics point inward and down, the center mic is also aimed down. Two additional mics are also generally used, one on either side of the orchestra, often at the outer edges. The center mic is routed equally to both stereo channels, with the right-side mics to the right and the left-side mics to the left.

Chapter 8

1. The controversial Jefferson Airplane album *Volunteers* was released in 1969. "We Can Be Together," the album's opening song, was pulled from the air after the FCC learned that Grace was singing the lyric, "Up against the wall, motherfucker." RCA had initially refused to allow the word *fuck* on the album, and held its release up for weeks before giving in. "Eskimo Blue Day," also on *Volunteers*, was also a point of contention with its repeated chorus line of "Compared to a stream, the American dream, doesn't mean shit to a tree."

2. The Echoplex, first made in 1959 and originally designed by Mike Bat-

tle, was a variable tape delay effect housed in a box. The tape speed and the distance between the record and playback heads determined the delay time, and the delayed sound could also be fed back into itself to create repeated echoes.

INDEX